UNWRAPPING THE
CIO

UNWRAPPING THE
CIO

Demystifying the Chief Information Officer Position

Wayne L. Anderson
Chief IT Strategist

Andrea Ravaioli
May 25TH, 2007
Montreal

iUniverse, Inc.
New York Lincoln Shanghai

Unwrapping The CIO
Demystifying the Chief Information Officer Position

Copyright © 2006 by Wayne L. Anderson

iUniverse books may be ordered through booksellers or by contacting:

iUniverse
2021 Pine Lake Road, Suite 100
Lincoln, NE 68512
www.iuniverse.com
1-800-Authors (1-800-288-4677)

The author has taken care in the preparation of this book, but makes no expressed or implied warranty of any kind and assumes no responsibility for errors or omissions. No liability is assumed for incidental or consequential damages in connection with or arising out of the use of the information or programs contained herein.

ISBN-13: 978-0-595-40058-4 (pbk)
ISBN-13: 978-0-595-84441-8 (ebk)
ISBN-10: 0-595-40058-2 (pbk)
ISBN-10: 0-595-84441-3 (ebk)

Printed in the United States of America

To Pam,
My partner in our bold mission to enter brave
new worlds during our life trek…and beyond.

Contents

What People Are Saying

"Unwrapping the CIO offers the reader a great perspective on the expectations and challenges facing the CIO in today's successful businesses, which will appeal to business and IT leaders alike. If you are an aspiring or existing CIO, Wayne Anderson provides the means to reflect on your own style and contribution to ensure that you are positioned to optimise your effectiveness in this crucial role."

Chris Rawson, Chief Information Officer
Lloyd's of London

"This book should be read by CIOs, the people who work with them, and those who aspire to the CIO role. Anderson has a unique approach to describing the skills that are necessary to be successful in this demanding position, and he outlines well the responsibilities and capabilities that are required to achieve success. Enjoy the read!"

Jim Fitzpatrick, Chief Information Officer
Intuit, Inc.

"This book provides much common sense and useful guidance for aspirant CIOs and those already in the role. Thought provoking and challenging in equal measures, it will inspire and help many Technology Leaders to continue to achieve against the backdrop of a rapidly changing corporate universe."

Simon La Fosse, Director, CIO Practice
Harvey Nash plc

"I found this book to be highly informative. It is written in an easy-to-follow style that draws you into its web of knowledge, and you come away from it richer for the experience. While painting an accurate picture of how difficult the CIO job is, it also gives hope that the position can be mastered. It is a must read for new CIOs or other senior managers wanting to grasp the position, and it is a good source manual for young information technology professionals wanting to prepare."

Randall Gannaway, Senior Vice President, Enterprise Infrastructure
Management
Sabre Holdings

"This book provided me with a 'walk in my shoes' experience without needing to live in an IT department for several weeks."

David Davis, Senior Vice President, Operations
Leap Communications

"The book provided a great deal of insight into a job that is very complex, very stressful, and yet very sought after. Anderson has written this book in a manner that makes it very easy to read and provides down-to-earth analogies, which provide clarity and humor. Reading it was like spending a week with a mentor for whom you have a great deal of respect. There is wisdom to be gained by reading this book that can be applied for your own gain, regardless of where you work in an organization. This is true even if you are an aspiring business partner or marketing representative."

Ron McGee, Manager, Information Technology
Fortune 500 Insurance Company

Acknowledgments

A book like this could never come to fruition without the help of a large number of people. Many people with whom I have worked over the years have provided me with the experiences that were the basis for this book. Many have actively participated in its creation.

Most important, I want to thank my wife, Pam, who played the role of editor, consultant, and, sometimes, conscience. She spent a large amount of time proofreading and helping me structure and format the final manuscript. In addition, she provided a great deal of encouragement and support during times when it felt difficult to move forward, when life appeared to get in the way.

Many people currently in the chief information officer's (CIO) position participated in my online study and were part of my professional business network. Their insights and experiences were valuable in providing real-world examples in the life of a CIO. Their words of wisdom have been distributed throughout the book.

Finally, many thanks go to the members of the Tulsa, Oklahoma, chapter of the National Speakers Association (NSA), who provided a wealth of encouragement, advice, and support. Their monthly fireside chats gave me invaluable insights. They also gave me access to hundreds of years of priceless experience.

Figures

Preface

What is the chief information officer (CIO) position really all about? What skills are needed to be successful in this job? Where does the CIO position belong in the organization? Why is it so difficult for business people to understand and communicate with the CIO and the people in the information technology (IT) department? Why do the challenges of the CIO seem so unique versus other positions in the company? Where does the IT department spend the money in its budget?

These are all questions I had when I became a divisional CIO for a major airline a number of years ago. (Actually, the divisional CIO title didn't exist back then, but the activities that that I was performing are considered CIO functions today.) I searched for books and seminars on the topic so that I could better understand the job and what I needed to do to be successful in the job. Unfortunately, all I could find were seminars and books on hardware, software, networks, software development techniques, and many other esoteric items unique to the IT profession. I had either already developed an expertise or had some level of familiarity with all these things. None of them really answered my questions.

I interacted with senior business people on a regular basis. Some of them became my peers as I progressed through the organization. Because I came up through the technical ranks of the organization, I did not fully understand the challenges that some of my peers were facing. There were many times that I did not understand them, and they clearly did not understand me. Later, I became a divisional CIO for a major insurance company, where I reported to the chief financial officer. With the insurance company, I worked closely with the top five or six people in the company, including the CEO. Although I had learned a lot from my previous position in the airline, I realized that there was still a *disconnect* between my understanding of what my position was and their knowledge of what they thought I should be doing. I continued to see the same disconnect even after I had reached the senior vice president level in a multibillion-dollar company.

There is a saying: "It's not the truth that hurts; it's the sudden realization of it!" I had a sudden realization that each person with whom I was interacting looked at me (and my position) from a different perspective. I was required to be a number of different people, depending on whom I was working with or talking to at any given time. I was required to have a different set of skills and to provide a different level of interaction for each person I encountered. That was when I decided that the CIO and the people who work with that person needed a book to help them understand the position and the people who perform that function. If you are a CIO, you need to understand the job in which you were placed. If you are a CEO, you need to better understand the position, challenges, and skill requirements of one of the key positions affecting your organization. If you are a CFO, you need to understand the position that consumes a great deal of the company's financial assets. If you are an IT professional, you need to understand why CIOs make some of the decisions they make. Even if you only interact with the CIO on a regular basis, you need to better understand the actions and behaviors of that person. That is how and why I chose to write *Unwrapping the CIO: Demystifying the Chief Information Officer Position*.

My hope is that this book will provide you with answers to many questions that I have had to learn through experience.

Enjoy!

Wayne L. Anderson
Tulsa, Oklahoma

Introduction

Chapter

"No problem exists that can withstand the assault of sustained thinking."
—Unknown

The objective of this chapter is to introduce new chief information officers (CIOs) to the role and provide some insight. In addition, this section outlines how current CIOs might benefit from reading this book. Finally, for anyone who is not currently a CIO and does not plan to become one, this chapter covers the other possible benefits that can come from reading this book. This is especially true for people who interact closely with the company's CIO.

First Things First: Don't Panic

My opening message to you, the chief information officer (CIO) of your organization, is that this is a unique and challenging opportunity. It will be exciting as you move into areas and make decisions that other executives do not experience. Although becoming a CIO may seem to be a daunting task, there are many tools available to help you succeed, including this book. It is my intention that this book act as your mentor in your new assignment.

It is a well-known fact among family, friends, and colleagues that I am a *Star Trek* fan and have been for many years. The *Star Trek* series contain both TV shows and movies. My favorite *Star Trek* movie seems to be an appropriate concept with which to open this book.

In this movie, there is a training session for a class of new Star Fleet cadets that takes place on a mock-up of the starship *Enterprise*. During the training mission, the cadet in command of this simulated version of the *Enterprise* is placed in a scenario that seems to be one of those "damned if you do, damned if you don't" situations. If she doesn't go into a particular area of outer space and save the starship *Kobayashi Maru*, the occupants of the ship will surely be doomed. If she does save the ship, she will cross into the infamous area of outer space known as the "neutral zone," thereby violating a somewhat-tenuous peace treaty. This will not only doom her ship and the starship that is in trouble, but also risk an intergalactic war. She decides that rescuing the ship is worth the risk. She crosses into the neutral zone, tries to rescue the ship, finds out it is a trap set by their formidable enemy, gets attacked, and is destroyed. Fortunately, it is only a simulation.

This testing scenario was called the *Kobayashi Maru*, more popularly known among young Star Fleet cadets as the no-win scenario. The scenario does not have a right or wrong answer. Instead, it is intended to test the stress tolerances, psychological makeup, and leadership skills—or character, if you will—of the cadet in command.

I realize that, at this point, your appointment to the position of CIO may seem like nothing more than a *Kobayashi Maru*. You may have heard that CIO really stands for "career is over." If you haven't, you will. This is not the case. It could, however, be a test of your character. At the very least, this opportunity will provide insight into the person that you are.

Captain James T. Kirk, the long-standing starship captain and one of the primary heroes in the *Star Trek* series, was the only cadet to beat the no-win scenario, essentially by changing the rules of the game.

You could likewise be considered a hero of the CIO community and beat the image that your career is over. Just like Kirk, you may need to change the rules a little. With the help of this book and the accompanying reference material, I believe you can, and will, win—even in no-win situations—and that you will become an outstanding CIO.

About This Book

I will provide you with several concepts in this book. It is not my intention to go into significant depth on any of these concepts or to help you become an expert in any one area. When applicable, I will provide references to more in-depth material on topics that may be of value to you.

My primary objective is to highlight and make you aware of as many aspects and dimensions of the of the CIO role as possible. I will challenge your process for thinking as an organization's CIO. Once you begin to understand your thought process and think critically about all these areas, you will become a more well-rounded and effective CIO.

I have organized the chapters to build on one another. In the second chapter, "What Is a CIO Anyway?" I offer a definition and description of the role of a chief information officer. In chapter 3, "MP is Normal," I present the idea that the CIO encompasses many roles, and that the role a CIO takes on at any given moment varies, depending on the situation or person with which the CIO is dealing. In the chapter "Unexpected Challenges," I discuss in-depth actions in which the CIO should be involved. Here we will explore some of the decisions and challenges that the CIO will face. I also present some techniques that will help you succeed in this position. The chapter "Your People" is designed to help the CIO with management and leadership challenges. For example, many CIOs do not have an information technology (IT) background or may never have managed IT professionals. As a result, they find it a challenge to mange technical people. In this chapter, I give you some management and leadership techniques that I have personally used over the years that have worked for me. I developed some of these techniques because I didn't have a book like this one to help me. I also thought it would be helpful to include a chapter entitled "Reference Material." In this chapter, I present some sources that may not be labeled as CIO reference sources, but that will certainly be helpful to CIOs. Other sources provide concepts or techniques that will help you succeed in your new job. Finally, I have created an appendix of informational tips that were given to me by a number of incumbent CIOs, which I call "Knowledge Nuggets." I have also created a glossary of terms and commonly used acronyms. Regardless of your technical background, it is virtually impossible to know every acronym from all of the areas under your auspices.

In researching this book, I have enlisted the feedback and advice of senior IT professionals who currently hold the position of CIO or are among the top 1 percent of IT leaders. I reference this feedback throughout the book and indicate the feelings of these respondents on various topics that are important to you. My hope is that their expertise and experiences will be valuable to you as you embark on this new challenge.

Who Should Read This Book

When I started writing this book, it was for people just placed in the role of CIO. I felt that those individuals might not be sure of all the various aspects of the position. Because I did not have such a book available to me, I wanted to help those individuals avoid the pitfalls with which I had become very familiar.

Since my initial writing—and with feedback from many supporters—I have expanded my audience. For example, people who currently hold the CIO position or professionals who are not CIOs as yet but who may be considering it as a career will also benefit from this book by gaining a better understanding of what the CIO does as well as tools to help them become successful in their endeavors.

Most organizations rely heavily on the information technology department to win in the marketplace. They rely on it to help them reduce costs, shorten the customer's value chain, more efficiently interact with providers and suppliers, and enhance the company's products and services. Therefore, the chief executive officer (CEO) can use this book to better understand the various characteristics of the CIO position and how it relates to the direction of the company. The partners of the CIO (i.e., the business heads of the other departments within the company, such as finance, marketing, etc.) can use this book to see how the services the CIO provides could enhance the products and services of their respective organizations.

All readers will have a better perspective of the unique interactions that are required for a CIO and their companies to succeed.

The Silver Bullet...

In the old stories about werewolves, the only way to eliminate a werewolf and end its rampage of terror was to shoot it with a silver bullet. (Of course, gaining the knowledge of this obscure solution and finding the silver bullet was always the real challenge.) The hero usually fashioned a silver bullet out of some esoteric piece of silver that was lying around.

If you are hoping to find the silver bullet that will solve all of your problems and answer all of your questions as a new CIO, forget it. It doesn't exist. The purpose of this book is to help you fashion the tools that you need to stand out as an insightful and knowledgeable CIO and to help you succeed in your new position.

Let's get started.

What Is a CIO Anyway?

Chapter 2

"The paradox of the human condition is that people, as a whole, are much the same yet individually are completely different"

—Unknown

Within corporations there are many job descriptions and positions. You could be employed as the chief financial officer (CFO), chief marketing officer (CMO), accountant, or in numerous other positions. So I guess you could say that the chief information officer is just another position in the company, right? Let's take a minute to examine that thought.

How many potential places on the corporate organization chart are you likely to find the CMO? How about the CFO? The CIO position can be found in numerous places in the organization chart.

How often do you find a C-level job (i.e., CEO, COO, CFO, CMO, etc.) that would report to another C-level position (other than to the CEO)? The CIO position sometimes reports to the CEO, sometimes the COO, sometimes the CFO, and in some organizations the CMO.

Just how many C-level positions could be split into multiple C-level positions? There are companies that split the CIO into two C-level positions, the chief information officer and the chief technology officer.

These are just a few characteristics that exist for the C-level job known as the chief information officer. This makes it difficult to create a succinct definition of a CIO. Yet we will pursue this challenge in this chapter. We will look at the various locations within an organization that your job could be placed. In addition, we will delve into the responsibilities of your position, regardless of the business model that defines your organizational location.

What Is a CIO? There's No Easy Answer

In general, it is easy to define most professions. If someone asks, "What is a computer programmer?" or "What is a retail store manager?" most people can usually answer that question.

But the problem with defining the CIO position is that it differs depending on the company in which you are working. In some companies, the CIO reports directly to the CEO and sits at the executive table (see figure 1).

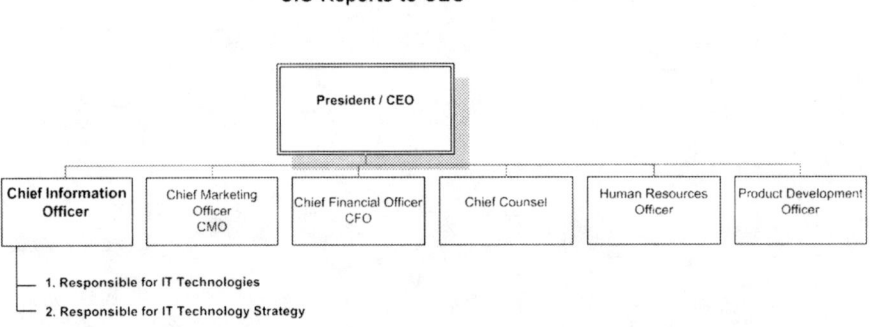

Figure 1. CIO reports directly to CEO.

Figure 2 shows that in other companies the CIO reports to someone who reports to the CEO (e.g., the CFO, the COO, etc.).

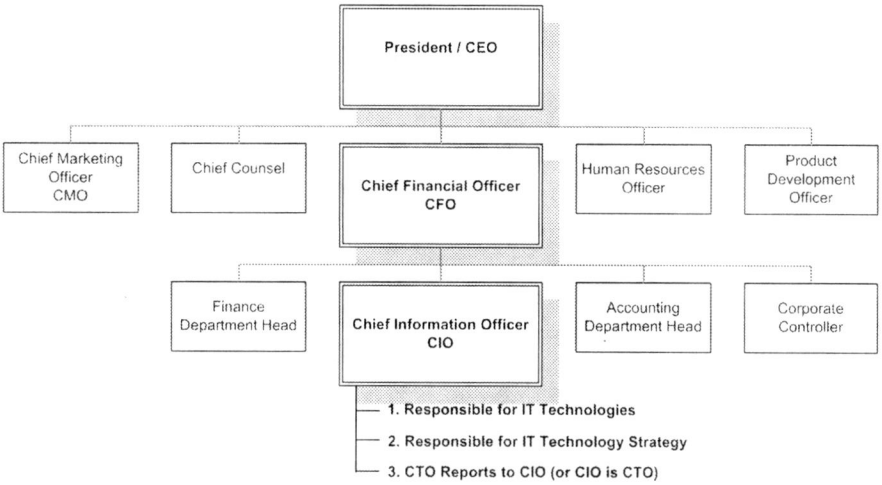

Figure 2. CIO reports to someone other than the CEO.

Figure 3 illustrates other companies in which CIOs only have the back-office application systems (i.e., payroll, accounting, etc.), while in still other companies, CIOs have all of the application systems and information system products.

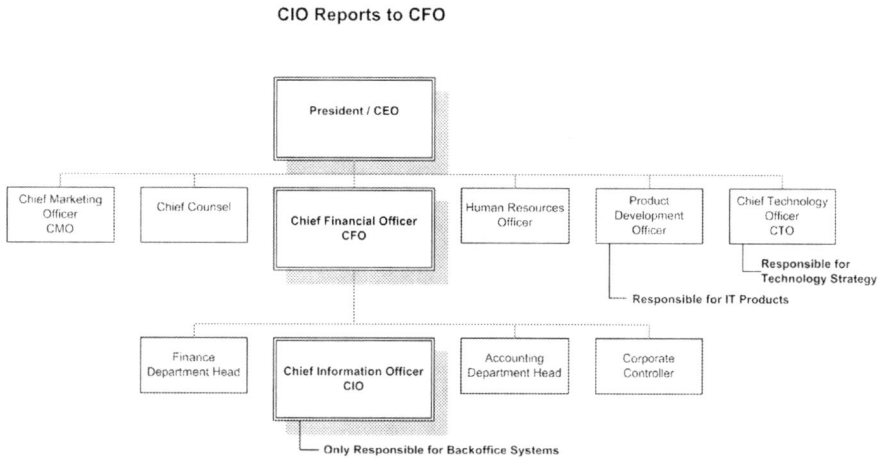

Figure 3. CIO is *only* responsible for back-office systems.

In the previous examples, the role of the CIO includes the role of the chief technology officer (CTO). However, in figure 4, the CIO and the CTO are different positions and they both report to the CEO.

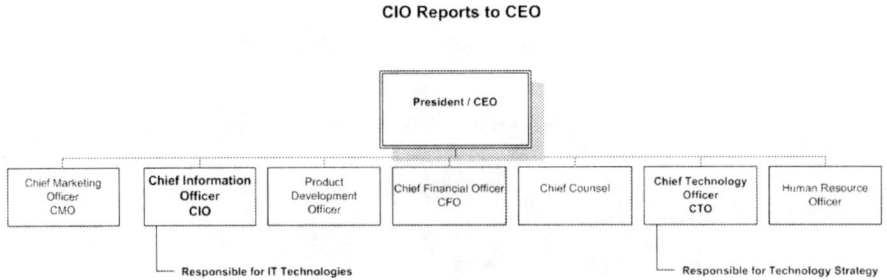

CIO Reports to CEO

Figure 4. The CIO and CTO are different positions.

In other organizations, they *are* considered the CTO and/or have the CTO reporting to them. Sometimes they have the data centers and computer operations functions in their organization. In other cases, the data center is in a separate department. In many organizations, the CIOs have other, non-IT organizations reporting to them. One of the most common non-IT organizations that I have seen the CIO responsible for is buildings and facilities. If this is the case, then the buildings and facilities become some of the assets under their auspices that will need a security program. (I will discuss more about this in the next chapter where I will cover security considerations.)

There are companies in some industries (e.g., financial services) that reserve the CIO title for the chief investment officer. In those companies, the person who manages the IT organization has a different title, most commonly called the chief technology officer (CTO).

"What is a CIO?" is not a question that can easily be answered without knowing the business model of the corporation in which the CIO resides.

Apart from any specific business model, there are some common responsibilities that every CIO is expected to perform. I have identified seven general categories into which, I believe, your responsibilities as a CIO will fall. They include the following:

Executive Team Member

- As CIO, you must be prepared to be a valued member of the executive team. You must participate in strategy-setting meetings and discussions. You must establish effective partnerships and working relationships with the entire senior management team; develop key internal relationships with senior management team members, including the CEO and board of directors; and work closely with internal senior management to ensure that you have a full understanding of their major technology needs and initiatives.

Strategic Technology Direction

- As CIO, you must also provide strategic technological direction and oversight. You must demonstrate exemplary abilities in strategic planning and overall business acumen. You will create the vision of your company for future use of information technology as a competitive weapon. Nearly 80 percent of CIOs who responded to my survey indicated that strategy development was the most important responsibility of the CIO. Of those surveyed, 90 percent indicated that they participate in their company's strategic-planning process.

- You must develop a robust understanding of business strategies and the resultant IT needs. You must determine the long-term corporate-wide information needs and develop a strategy to address those needs, including systems development, hardware acquisition, and integration of mainframe and client/server applications. You will be required to identify and manage the strategic enterprise-level IT initiatives that will significantly impact the business, improve operational efficiencies, provide access to information, and increase competitive advantage. You must contribute to and provide thought leadership for long-range business-planning processes and provide assurance that investments in technical solutions, architecture, and tools are closely aligned with IT and business objectives. This leadership will enable the business to meet its strategic growth objectives.

- You must maintain market intelligence to identify and leverage opportunities as they relate to IT. This includes being aware of current and future opportunities and developing new products and relationships that will continue to assist the company in maintaining its competitive advantage.

You will need to understand and recognize changes and trends in information technology and interpret their impact on your business.

Technology Leadership

- As CIO, you must lead the IT activities. You will be the senior solutions executive responsible for the direction of systems and technologies. You will have to create seamless and integrated fact-based management decision systems through which the senior leadership team will be able to more effectively direct the business strategies and plans. You will be responsible for rationalizing the value of the existing IT landscape. It will be your job to manage the technology architecture, applications development, package solutions evaluation and selection, database management, network communications, end-user computing, operations delivery, and project management. You will need to create an effective model for capital project funding and IT governance priority with the business. You will create the technology vision and definition of the future platforms required to support the enterprise, ensuring the technology infrastructure enhances the clients' interactions with suppliers and customers.

- You must assess the current IT systems in place and develop, implement, and evolve the tactical and strategic IT plans. You will be responsible for the development of more robust management information systems as well as reengineering the business processes that use those systems. Not all systems will be new. Therefore, you will also be responsible for fully integrating recently implemented systems into all frontline business activities, as well as the existing infrastructure and systems portfolio.

- You must develop and support data warehouse, query and reporting, Online Analytical Processing (OLAP), financial analytic applications, customer/market analytic applications, scorecards, and dashboards.

- You must provide for the operation of the company's global voice and data networks. In addition, your management oversight will include the efficient and effective operation of the company's data center(s).

- You must give support to the worldwide mobile workforce of sales and consultants and provide development and support for the laptop, desktop, and Web-based product environments.

- You must review, approve, and prioritize all major technology purchases, development projects, and system implementation initiatives, ensuring business value-added emphasis.

- You must assure the integrity of the corporate data, proprietary information, and related intellectual property through information security and access management.

- You must integrate the information technology functions of newly acquired companies in a timely and efficient manner—if your company has a strategy of growth though acquisition. In addition, you will be leading the successful technology integration of newly combined existing businesses, in both infrastructure and people. This may include the consolidation of call centers, data centers, and so forth.

IT Organization Management

- As CIO, you must develop and manage the global IT organization. You will have management responsibility for a global technology organization, plus any additional shared IT resources. As a senior management team member, you will need to influence the management committee and provide input on corporate-wide decisions.

- You must develop, execute, and manage a vision for rolling out products within the organization. You must identify the need for designing, coordinating, implementing, and evaluating the effectiveness of the business's IT policies, procedures, and systems to ensure effective and cost-efficient information resources to support and advance the company's strategic and tactical objectives. You must put together the plans for integrating and leveraging IT assets across the company to seamlessly provide shared products and services to both your internal business partners and your external customers.

- You must establish, rationalize, and manage the multimillion-dollar annual IT budget and serve as a member of the capital expenditure committee. It will be your responsibility to ensure that the IT team delivers reliable, value-added business solutions in a cost-effective and timely manner.

- You must provide motivation, leadership, and development of the technical staff. You will need to be skillful in aligning the employees, using their skills to achieve a cohesive team environment. In most cases, you will be building and managing a team of experienced, talented IT professionals. This means that your responsibilities will include motivation, training, recruitment, retention, and career development. Keep in mind that you may be leading a geographically dispersed organization of information technology professionals who reside in multiple countries.

- You must develop current knowledge, best practices, and the future vision of technology across the company. The value added from this effort will enhance the company's competitive position, meet the business goals, reduce operating costs, and increase the efficiency of the IT environment.

Business Partnership

- You must support the corporate business unit development and strategic planning initiatives. This means you need to provide the highest level of collaboration with product marketing and finance, as well as the other business development functions in determining the overall information systems approaches and priorities.

- You must provide coordination with the other functional areas to achieve established objectives in technology and information. You must partner with the organization to capture future benefits from information technology implementations. You will need to develop and enhance the system plans to provide strong cross-functional relationships throughout the company. You will need to position IT to participate in all interdepartmental systems development efforts. You must ensure that the business' overall investment in IT achieves its potential.

- You must position the information office at the front end of evaluating and planning potential acquisitions.

- You must develop key external relationships with technology vendors, industry analysts, external business partners, prospects, and customers. It will be your responsibility to develop and manage external service provider relationships. You must be intimately involved in the development of technology contractual agreements for the delivery of technical products and services in conjunction with the company's strategic sourcing.

IT Consultant and/or Advisor

- You must serve as the company's principal information technology advisor. You will need to act as one of the principal technology advisors to the management committee regarding the present and future uses of technology as a strategic competitive weapon, and you must guide senior management's understanding and effective sponsorship of IT initiatives. You will interface with senior management to effectively translate and implement IT needs across the organization. You must envision—and then realize—the optimum utility of IT by assisting senior leaders in recognizing where new technology would enhance performance while transforming or supporting business operations. You must make sure that enterprise-wide issues and considerations are raised and are part of the corporate technical decision-making process.

- You must become a key internal knowledge resource for the company's products, positioning, and customer base where IT products and business products align. You must provide expert-level technology consulting to the enterprise and affiliates and facilitate technology decision making. You also need to serve as liaison between the company's firms to ensure that the enterprise understands the overall technical direction and standards.

- You must effectively represent the company to the high-technology industry, investment market, government, associations, and community groups. You will also be required to represent the company at customer and business partner events as the company's technology expert and visionary. This will essentially make you the information technology voice of the company to the outside community.

Business Process Improvement

- You must improve the business processes for efficiency and effectiveness.

When you compare the job of a CIO with other positions, the CIO position will seem intimidating on a good day. A number of corporations use information technology as a strategic weapon in the marketplace. That provides you with the opportunity to have a strong leadership position within your company. To accomplish these formidable responsibilities, you will need to wear many different hats and display many different corporate personalities. In the next chapter, we will explore those personalities and will begin to understand their importance to you, as the CIO, and to your company.

MP Is Normal

Chapter 3

"Talking to yourself is normal. You should only be concerned if you get into an argument with yourself and then proceed to lose the argument!"
—Wayne L. Anderson

People are funny. No one ever likes to be labeled, but everyone labels everyone else. Most people label for a mental reference of another person. The label is usually a single term intended to describe that person's personality. You might hear people say things like, "My boss is a tyrant," or "She's really aggressive"; "He's bigger than life," "She's as meek as a mouse," or "He's a bully," and so on. We say these things (sometimes overtly, sometimes in the privacy of our own thoughts) as though one simple term could fully describe something as complex as the human personality. We do this because it is easier for us to think of people as one dimensional; it's easier to recall that person. Many scholars call this "totalizing." They define *totalizing* as thinking and acting as if a single aspect of a person is the totality of that person. In reality, a person could be labeled a tyrant by a subordinate and at the same time be considered a saint by a loving daughter. Their son or possibly their favorite sibling could consider them a great coach. So if a person has many different labels given to them by many individuals, does it mean that they have multiple personalities? Absolutely.

Let's say we placed ten people in a room around a rectangular table. We asked each person sitting along the sides and the person at the far end of the table to silently describe the person at the head of the table. Each of them will give that person the label they believe best describes them. But, in reality, each of them only describes their bias and their filtered view of that person. Their collective filters, however, would form a more complete description of that person's personality.

An individual's personality is much like a painting on a canvas. A painting is made up of many brushstrokes that form the final creation. Some strokes are thin; some are thick; some are straight; and some are curved. If we only saw one brushstroke of the *Mona Lisa*, we would surely miss out on a fantastic master-piece. We can only enjoy a work of art by viewing the results of all the brush-strokes together. In this chapter, we will observe the amazing position of the CIO. We will form an understanding of the many brushstrokes that shape the distinc-tive and unique professional known as the chief information officer.

What Is MP?

You often hear talk about people having a "split" personality. Of course there is no medical evidence that supports the fact that anyone could truly have a split personality. There *is* medical evidence to support the existence of people with multiple personalities (MP).

The standard definition of the condition called Multiple Personality Disorder or MPD is offered by the *Diagnostic and Statistical Manual of Mental Disorders* (DSM), which calls it "the existence within the individual of two or more distinct personalities, each of which is dominant at a particular time" (APA, 2000). Almost unheard of in popular culture until the 1950s, MPD was thrust into the public's consciousness in Corbett Thigpin and Hervey Cleckley's 1957 book, *The Three Faces of Eve*, that was made into an award-winning film. At that time, according to Thigpin and Cleckley, it was assumed that having multiple personalities was a rarity in psychopathology. Turns out, it is not. There have been over 40,000 cases diagnosed since the early 1970s.

Not all displays of multiple personalities are the result of a disorder or pathological condition. For example, it is the job of a character actor to exhibit many personalities as a normal part of their profession. Actors can play as many as fifty to sixty roles during the span of their career. A career that is by no means easy. Actors might perform in a commercial one week, do a small part in a movie the following week, and have a major role in an episode of a television series the next. Each role reveals the characteristics of a unique personality. These personalities— although authentic in the depiction—are usually fictional characters.

You were made Chief Information Officer. At that precise moment, unbeknownst to you, a number of new personalities were instilled within your persona. Each of these personalities, unlike those portrayed by actors, are very real. Fortunately, however, they do not represent a pathological condition.

As you work with other people in the organization, they will all see you differently. Each person will visualize a distinct personality. Individually, they will expect each personality to be different and produce different results. They will also respond to your products and services in a variety of ways. As CIO, sometimes you will need to be a strategist, sometimes a tactician, sometimes a technology wizard, and sometimes a salesperson, just to name a few of your potential personalities. At times (e.g., when talking with the investment community), your

CEO will expect you to be many of these personalities at the same time. You will be required to take on numerous personalities during your tenure as CIO. Therefore, for you, having multiple personalities is normal.

Let's examine more closely some of the more prevailing personalities with which you will need to deal.

CIO the Technologist or CTO—MP within MP

The technologist personality is like having MP within MP!

You may be an officer of the company and be an astute businessperson. In most companies, as CIO you will be expected to manage the company's technological environment (some companies have a chief technology officer that does this and does not report to the CIO). You must leverage the technology to add value to the company's strategic business direction. The technologist needs to be a dominant personality.

List the top three issues that you deal with most in your job.

1   *"Never allowing myself to get caught up in only being a CIO."*
2   *"Always being diligent."*
3   *"Never thinking I am the best at what I do."*

Patrick O'Neal
Griffin and O'Neal Staffing

There are many types of technology; you are expected to have some level of knowledge about all of them. Depending on the company that you are in, you may need to have more knowledge of some types of technology than others. If you change companies, you may need a completely different set of technical skills and knowledge. In any case, all these types of technologies are disciplines within themselves. Think of it like having separate personalities within the technologist personality.

I will not attempt to give you a lesson on all of the types of technology you may encounter during your tenure as CIO. There may not be a warehouse large enough to house all of the volumes of text that would be required, and I am thoroughly convinced that I don't have enough years left on this planet to write about all of them. And technology changes so rapidly that anything that I write would be obsolete before it went to print. Suffice it to say that a great deal has already been written on each of the subjects mentioned below, as well as many types of technology that I will not mention.

Understand that, as CIO, people are going to expect you to have some understanding of various types of technology. They are going to expect—and rightfully so—that you will select the technology necessary to move the corporate strategies forward and support the accomplishment of corporate objectives. For example, if your corporate strategies focus on mergers and acquisitions, then your technology decisions and strategies should be concerned with integrating information technology environments that might be very different. You may have to merge dissimilar data center environments that are geographically dispersed. If your company has a strategy to provide the lowest-price product, then you may need to consider an information technology strategy that moves development work offshore. And so on. Regardless of your technical background and your company's business strategy, you need to be prepared to play this role.

Let's examine some of the types of technology that make up the technologist personality.

Applications Development

By far applications development is the most important area of your technologist personality. The bottom line of all of your efforts, the essence of all of your personalities, and the principal value that you will bring to your company is to produce an IT product. You do that through your applications development efforts.

Nowadays the effective use of information can make or break a company. In the past information systems were just one of the business tools to help get the job done. Now many products in many companies are information technology systems. These companies realize that if information is managed intelligently, it can generate additional revenue, gain market share, and enhance the business processes. Your effectiveness in systems applications development will play a key role in adding value to your enterprise.

Application Languages

Most people who know multiple languages and use that knowledge in their chosen profession are called interpreters. As a CIO, this is your interpreter personality, because you will definitely need to know about multiple languages.

Should you use Java or C? Should it be C or C++? Will COBOL be the language of choice or should it be Assembler? Or maybe even a special form of Assembler called TPF? Maybe XHTML would be a better choice than XML or HTML. What is that LINUX thing, anyway?

These are decisions that you must make, depending on the environment in which you are developing information technology solutions. If your development is primarily Web based, you may choose a set of application program languages that best support that environment. Likewise, if your environment is primarily high transaction mainframe based, a different set of languages may be more appropriate. To complicate the situation, you may have a hybrid environment where midrange, server-level hardware nor mainframes are dominant. Here the two environments will need to play well together. You will need to consider a set of languages that interface well together. For example, it may be appropriate to have an operating system like Linux running in both hardware environments so that the C programming language can be used on both platforms.

The appropriate language or set of languages should be based on the strategic direction of the company. You must understand that direction and then be the interpreter of the appropriate language(s) to sustain that direction.

Web Services

I started in the business of IT over thirty years ago. Punch cards were king! We were amazed at how fast technology was changing. I mean, just about the time that we thought we had things figured out, computers became so fast that water was pumped into the CPUs to cool them down. Water inside the computer, no way! Yes, water inside of the computer. At that point, we never thought we would be able to keep up with the technology changes. Guess what? Things haven't changed (see "Things Are Changing (and Will Continue to Change) Faster Than You" in chapter 4).

Web Services is one of the latest changes with an extreme impact on the way you, the CIO, will do your job. It has completely changed the way we think about distributed computing. Eric Newcomer, in his book *Understanding Web Services,* says, "Once the world becomes Web service enabled, all kinds of new business paradigms, discussion groups, interactive forums, and publishing models will emerge to take advantage of this new capability" (Newcomer, 2002). The idea of taking a technology like the Web and creating a layer of abstraction above it creates an entire new world of capability.

You may want to devote time to understanding Web services technology, since this has the possibility of significantly enhancing your information office service offerings. It is my opinion that your technologist personality could be *shortchanged* if you don't devote some time to the understanding of Web services. Learning these concepts will help ensure that your technologist personality remains healthy.

Infrastructure

Generally, infrastructure refers to the physical buildings, data centers, the computers within the data centers, data and voice networks, and, sometimes, the help desk functions. In many of the business models that we previously discussed, the CIO is responsible for some or all of these functions. Whether or not you have direct responsibility for these functions, it is imperative that you understand these areas and appreciate the interrelationships of the infrastructure components. A solid infrastructure is essential to the successful delivery of your products. You need to know whether the infrastructure supports, enhances, or, unfortunately, hinders your delivery objectives.

Networks

Remember when *networking* meant staying connected with a series of key people who you called when you needed help in getting things done? Well, now you have to expand your definition a bit.

I remember when managing the networks only meant the data network. As a result of the convergence and integration of voice and data, the CIO is increasingly becoming responsible for both the voice and data networks. Think about it…You can retrieve your e-mails from your telephone. You can receive your voicemails in your e-mail inbox. Let's not forget that you can retrieve both your e-mails and your voicemails as well as access your company's Web site with your cell phone. Networks have become an integral part of doing business, and they are vital to your organization.

Your technologist personality provides solutions that will depend on the network utility. I call it a utility because it is a component of the infrastructure, and, therefore, your company will depend on it like a utility. When you enter a conference room and flip the light switch, for example, how often do you think about whether the power plant is up and running? Or whether the cables, repeaters, and switches between you and the power plant are connected properly, or whether the light will come on? I would bet never. Of course, your levels of consciousness will change if the light doesn't come on. That is the same way your business partners will think about the voice and data networks (and all of the infrastructure components for that matter). They will be accessing your products and services from all over the planet. When they do, they expect the network services to be there. But you can bet that their level of consciousness will definitely change if it is not there!

Software

One online encyclopedia[1] defines computer programs as

> A series of instructions that a computer can interpret and execute; programs are also called software to distinguish them from hardware, the physical equipment used in data processing. These programming instructions cause the computer to perform arithmetic and logical operations or comparisons (and then take some additional action based on the comparison) or to input or output data in a desired sequence.

Operating systems, commercial off-the-shelf (COTS) software, middleware, firmware, in-house computer programs, available objects, as well as the legacy systems exposed via Web services are all types of software of which you need to be aware. Your ability to employ this software to achieve the corporate goals is important.

Think of software as a key corporate asset that should be managed like any other corporate asset. When you think of the intellectual property (IP) contained in your company's internal software, software could be considered the most important asset. Depending on the business model of your company (e.g., insurance, finance, etc.), your company's products *are* the software. Later, I will discuss the concept of managing your systems through a life cycle (see the section "CIO the

---

[1] *See* Encyclopedia Reference on the Yahoo!® Education Web site.

Asset Manager"). At this point, suffice it to say that you must think of the company's software as more than just a collection of programs.

The people in your company expect you to know about all of the software both inside and outside of your company. They are going to question the existence, stability, validity, cost, and value of virtually every software program. If they don't, then *you* should question whether that piece of software is at the end of its useful life cycle.

There is a myriad of software in the marketplace that is not used in your company. In that case, you shouldn't care about it, right? Rest assured that during lunch, someone in your company will talk with a friend from another company about one of those software packages, or read about it in a trade magazine, or hear about it during a commercial break on the latest rerun of *Friends*. Their immediate reaction will be to call you so that you can explain why that software is not in your arsenal, since it will obviously solve every problem in the company. And, besides, you're the technology expert; you should know about these things. At this point you will experience an increased level of stress.

Remember that a part of your CTO persona is to understand any type of software that may help move your company in the appropriate direction. Although your primary source for this information will be your vendor partners, it will not be the only source. You should also understand that your business partners are savvier about systems today than ever before. You may want to have your technical "wizards" investigate and validate whether the software your business partner suggested is worth pursuing. If nothing else, it will help reduce your stress level.

Hardware

In the past when people talked about blades, they were referring to the razor they used to shave with that morning. When we talked about handheld items, we were referring to radios or calculators. There were only a couple of companies that made handheld computers, and the number of models a company made could be listed on one hand. It might seem that I am dating myself, but it really was not that long ago.

Think about what it is like today. Think about the different types of personal digital assistants (PDAs) that exist. Then think about the amount of software that exists for each PDA and the types of networks that can be used to exchange information. But, of course, we have just barely begun our review of hardware types.

Let's take it up a notch to the desktop. Of course, it could be a laptop. Again, we have a mind-boggling assortment of hardware, an astronomical display of software, and an impressive choice of cable and wireless connection alternatives. Since the hardware concerns are a part of your technologist personality, you must also consider things such as common office environment policies, software-updating scenarios, hardware standards, and refresh schedules, as well as synchronizing these machines with the servers and mainframes. You may have to consider whether to buy small, unintelligent desktop devices and run thin versions of the software. This will require having an architecture where the intelligence resides on the server. Or perhaps the desktop should contain the intelligence to support your knowledge, which could—if not managed properly—cause your hair color to become significantly lighter while you try to keep the myriad of software versions updated and in sync with the rest of your architecture.

Speaking of servers and mainframes, just exactly how do you know which is which? It used to be quite simple. The mainframe was very large and expensive and could perform very sophisticated multiprocessing. It had large databases, complex security, large, complicated networks, and an extremely fast operating system. The servers, on the other hand, had a very small footprint, were extremely inexpensive, and usually processed one program at a time. They had questionable security, fast but unreliable operating systems, and rudimentary hardwired networking. That was not that long ago. Today mainframes are smaller (many of them are now called servers), and servers are larger. All other aspects of their respective architectures look a lot alike. So, I ask again, how can you tell which is which?

It doesn't matter how you answer that question. In most organizations, as CIO you will also be the CTO. This will be true whether or not you have the official title of CTO. You will be thought of as senior management's technology guru. The majority of the current CIOs that I surveyed had a background in information technology before they were placed in their positions. Fortunately, there is a high probability that you will also have a background in IT. If that is the case, these issues are not foreign to you. I would bet that your experience and expertise was limited to a particular set of hardware or a specific architectural platform. I would also guess that there were one (or maybe two) operating systems with which you became familiar. Unfortunately, you no longer have the luxury of being hardware and operating system myopic. You will not be required to be an expert, but you will need to be aware of the plethora of hardware and software architectures. You must understand how technology is changing and whether the new features and functions are consistent with your business and technology strategies.

This may seem like a daunting task. It won't be if you make sure that you rely heavily on your technical wizards to keep you up-to-date. This is the primary reason for developing strong relationships with your vendors. They are a great source of education on technology changes. Your relationships with your vendors need to go beyond infrequent communication about nebulous charges on your current bill and/or the ritual quarterly sales call meetings. You should think about having the proper level of nondisclosure agreements. This will allow you to have open discussions that will ensure they understand your overall direction and you understand their technology roadmaps.

The Data Asset

Approximately thirty years ago, Dr. Richard Nolan, in his book *Managing the Data Resource,* suggested that data is a corporate resource. He suggested that the characteristics of a resource are cost, value, and scarcity. Therefore, like materials, buildings, and humans, to a corporation, data is also a resource. Resources are also assets of the corporation. That means that data is also a corporate asset. Since data is an asset, it should be managed through an asset life cycle like the other resources. It should be planned, acquired, employed, and retired, just as you do with other corporate resources (see below, "CIO the Asset Manager"). In addition, you should manage your data resources similar to the way a human resources department manages the people resource (Nolan, 1974).

I had just been appointed to the newly created position of data administrator at Kimberly-Clark Corporation when Dr. Nolan's book was released. I thought it was one of the most profound books ever written. I was extremely excited about the concept. I told everyone that would listen how we needed to manage data as a resource. A select few understood and agreed with me. The rest simply thought I had finally lost my mind.

Now I believe that data is more than just *a* resource. I think that data is the *most important* resource in a corporation. Without it, you could not effectively manage any of the other resources. As CIO the technologist, you need to understand the life cycle of data. You need to understand how to plan for data like you plan for the hiring of people or the materials that you need in manufacturing. You need to acquire the data that the corporation needs. Not all of the data the corporation needs to compete effectively is contained within the corporation. So you will need to provide access to external data as well as internal data. You need to employ the data. In other words, make sure that the data is efficiently stored in databases. The databases need to be structured so that the people within the corporation that need the data have easy access to it. Yet that access cannot be too easy for everyone. You will also need to make sure that the data is appropriately protected. Only the proper people should have access to the databases. The data needs to be protected from intruders that may want to steal, alter, or manipulate the data resource, either intentionally or unintentionally. You will also need to retire the outdated data that could provide erroneous information. If you do not manage this outdated data properly, it could be detrimental to your corporation.

I will end the discussion of the technologist persona with one of the most important aspects of the CIO's job, managing the data resource. As CIO, you need to manage the corporation's data just like you manage its cash, people, and buildings. Structure your organization to effectively support this resource. Most of all, understand that data is used to create information. Information is used to make decisions. Decisions establish strategy and courses of action. Consider what could happen to the direction of your company if the underlying data is incorrect, altered, or missing.

CIO the Strategist

"However good our futures research may be, we shall never be able to escape from the ultimate dilemma that all our knowledge is about the past, and all our decisions are about the future."

—Ian Wilson

In today's business environment of complexity, uncertainty, globalization, and rapid change, the chief information officer is increasingly participating in setting the strategy for the organization. Generally, the CIO will be involved in all aspects of strategy development. Close to 80 percent of incumbent CIOs in my survey said that this is the most significant aspect of their job. Like being a technologist, being a strategist should also be a dominant personality within your CIO persona.

Strategies may be the result of mergers and acquisitions, the establishment of global operations, the movement into new markets, the communication of information systems strategy and direction to investors, all of the above...and more. The responsibility of the CIO has moved from focusing on data center operations and programming to working with the CEO and the executive team to creatively design growth opportunities for the company. This personality is the visionary. To succeed as CIO, you will need to understand all aspects of the business and the strategic framework that the corporation uses for analyzing the uncertainties and be able to use persuasion and negotiating skills to influence others.

Once a hockey player was asked during an interview how he was able to outperform the other players so consistently. His response was, "Most players go to the spot on the ice where the puck is…I go to where it's going to be." In today's fast-paced world of business and commerce, executives have to think about where the puck is going to be. It is not about where the competition is but where they are going to be; it is not where the market is, but where it is going to be; it is not where technology is, but where it is going to be. The best method for staying a step ahead is through the development of astute strategies. These strategies should help make the unseen future visible. You, the CIO, will need to understand those strategies, participate in the development of those strategies, and develop similar strategies for the information office that are consistent with the business strategies.

List the top three issues that you deal with most in your job.

1   *"Staying focused and aligned with business."*
2   *"Staying strategic, not technical or tactical when working with peers."*
3   *"Delivering on the IT value proposition to enable the business success."*

Steve Printz, CIO

In their book *The Strategy-Focused Organization*, authors Robert S. Kaplan and David P. Norton write that a study of 275 portfolio managers concluded that the ability to execute strategy was more important than the quality of the strategy itself (Kaplan and Norton, 2001). You, as the CIO, will have a significant role in the execution of your organization's strategy since, more than likely, a great deal of the strategy will involve information systems and automation. We will go into more depth later about execution. For now, let's look at some of the ways in which you will contribute to and/or participate in the business strategies.

Mergers and Acquisitions

The merger and acquisition activity today is mind-boggling. Companies use mergers, acquisitions, and divestitures for a variety of reasons. Some companies use them to gain market share. Other companies make acquisitions to eliminate the competition. Many companies use these actions to obtain new products and services. Other companies use mergers and acquisitions to enlarge their distribution channels. In any case, the actions of the CIO and their team could make or break a strategic merger. One of the most difficult (if not *the* most difficult) activities during a merger is that integration of the information systems. I have been involved in several mergers, acquisitions, and consolidations. Investing helped me most in understanding the impact of the information systems environment on company mergers.

For years I have invested in equities. Fortunately, I have been fairly successful in my investing endeavors, and I have generally made a profit on the stocks that I buy and sell. A friend once told me that he thought that I was just lucky in the market. I told him how, at the time, I was spending approximately fifteen hours per stock in research and investigation of the company before I purchased the stock. I would read the annual reports, news articles, management comments, and 10-K filings. Then I would decide if the stock met my personal investment criteria, and, if so, I would make the purchase. I don't need to spend nearly as much time as I used to spend on research because of all of the electronic information and online access available today. I still cover all of the same basic information before making an investment; I just spend less time doing it.

My friend was impressed but curious about why I would read something as boring as a 10-K report. The Security and Exchange Commission requires a company to make these filings annually to report on the operations of the company. Some companies use this filing in place of an annual report. I told my friend how I learned a great deal about the company's operations, business model, competition, and general market climate from the 10-K filing. One of the most important things I learned in investing was the impact of mergers and acquisitions on a company's operations.

In reading about mergers and acquisitions in the 10-K report, one of the surprising things that I found out was the number of times that the integration of computer and information systems was mentioned as a possible hindrance to the success of the merger. There always seemed to be references to computer system integration as something that slowed down the progress of the newly merged company. That always intrigued me.

One of the companies in which I was interested in making an investment was a healthcare company. While I was reading its 10-K filing, I came across the following statement under the section entitled "Items That May Impact Future Operations" (I have removed all references to the name of the company and the companies that were acquired):

*The company has completed a number of significant acquisitions since 1996. Since the relevant dates of acquisition, the company has worked extensively on the integration of the acquired businesses. The company has also completed significant work on the integration of an additional business. The company expects to begin its integration of the most recent company during the remainder of the year. The company is continuing the consolidation of these acquired operations into its operations, which will require considerable expenditures and a significant amount of management time. Due to the complex nature of the merger integration process, particularly the information systems designed to serve these businesses, the company may temporarily experience increases in claims inventory or other service-related issues that may negatively affect the company's relationship with its customers and contribute to increased attrition of such customers. **The success of these acquisitions will, among other things, also require the integration of a significant number of the employees into the company's existing operations and the completion of the integration of separate information systems.** No assurances can be given regarding the ultimate success of the integration of these acquisitions into the company's business.*

The following is a quote out of the 10-K report of a software development company that had merging with a competitor that filled a strategic niche in the company's product offerings (I have removed all references to the name of the company and the acquired companies):

There are significant organizational and product integration risks related to any future business combination.

In addition to its acquisition of the company, we have made, and may in the future make, acquisitions of, mergers with, or significant investments in, businesses that offer complementary products, services and technologies. There are risks involved in these activities, including but not limited to:

- *The possibility that we will pay more than the value it derives from the acquisition;*

- *The difficulty of integrating the operations and personnel of the acquired businesses;*
- *The possibility that all aspects of the integration are not completed or that all of the anticipated synergies of the acquisition are not realized: the potential product liability associated with selling the acquired company's products;*
- *And the potential disruption of our ongoing business and the distraction of management from our business.*

These factors could have a material adverse effect on our business, results of operations or financial position, especially for a large acquisition.

This particular 10-K did not mention "computer systems" directly. Further investigation of the phrase "integrating the operations and personnel" revealed that the most significant operations to be integrated were the application systems, data centers, and operating system software. Amazingly enough, most of the business operations were extremely compatible with the acquiring company's business operations.

As the CIO, you will need to be intimately involved with the merger and acquisition activities of your company. One of the most complicated integration activities is the information systems environment. If a key strategy of your company is to grow through acquisition (which is not uncommon these days), then your involvement becomes a critical responsibility. Your information system integration strategy and plans—and the subsequent execution of those plans—could have a decisive impact on the success of the merger. Your participation in the merger and acquisition action could, and will, have an impact on future business operations.

Global Operations

Information technology is a critical enabler and many times the key driver of a company's global business expansion. The Internet eliminates the age-old restrictions of time, space, and location. It allows companies of all sizes to compete in the global marketplace. Electronic commerce provides the opportunity for transactions to be executed from anywhere on the planet. Internet-based electronic commerce is expected to have a major impact on the way companies do business worldwide. As a result, more and more companies are developing global marketing strategies. An alignment and integration of both local and worldwide computer information systems and business strategies is essential. This integration is especially critical to the success of multinational firms in the highly competitive global market. Internet technology has no regard for national or international borders. To improve the entire value chain, companies with global operations have developed electronic links with suppliers, customers, and business partners all over the globe. It is imperative that your strategist personality be involved with the development, integration, and implementation of the technology portion of the company's global expansion and operation strategies.

New Markets

Entering new markets is one of the most exciting endeavors on which your company will embark. Aggressive entry into the right new markets could make the senior management team look like geniuses to the investment community. In many instances, a company can energize a complacent workforce when it enters a new market or introduces new products and services. The development and execution of these strategies will require a great deal from the information systems organization—and your strategic personality.

Customer-centered innovation and competitive-pricing pressures will also drive a company to new development and provide access to new markets. In many cases the market is brand-new. History shows that innovation is an expansion or variation of an existing idea or approach. Many industry leaders, like Amazon.com, were not the first to create the products and services for which they are currently the leaders. But Amazon.com was the first *online* bookstore. Likewise, your company may not be the first to create the innovation that is in your new market strategy. It may just be the first to create the new product or service. Whatever the case, as the CIO strategist, you must understand the new market penetration strategy and integrate your technology solutions to enable those strategies to succeed.

Investor Relations

Information technology is becoming so pervasive that it is having a significant impact on a company's strategy and operations, and, therefore, stock price and investor relations. It is not unusual for the CIO to be appointed as an officer of the company. As a matter of fact, it is becoming standard. As an officer, you will find yourself answering questions at the company's annual meeting of stockholders. Investors are concerned with shareholder value. They feel that they get value when the company moves toward the top of its industry peer group. You should be prepared to field questions from the gentle, passive, aggressive, or irate stockholder. You may be forced to present two or three of your personalities, depending on where the investor perceives your company to be on that scale. The questions may be directed toward the costs associated with new technology (CIO the Financial Manager), the use of technology to penetrate a new market (CIO the Strategist), how the new technology-based product or service works (CIO the Technologist), or how protected their technology environment is (CIO the Security Chief). When participating in the investor relations portion of your strategy persona, recognize that you may need to call on some of your other personalities as well.

If someone asked you, "What is a CIO?" how would you define the position?

"The strategist and manager for integrating the IT systems with business strategy."

Terry Miller
Professor of eCommerce
Kaplan University

One final word for the strategist persona. There are a number of different approaches to strategy development (e.g., scenario planning, balanced scorecard, etc.). You need to find out which approach your company uses, learn the fundamentals, determine how your information office will help develop the organization's strategy, and then execute it. It is imperative that you develop a process for integrating the information systems strategy directly into the business strategy. By doing so you are assured that your organization focuses on things important to the success of the corporation.

CIO the Tactician

It will not be enough for you to be a strategist. You will need to take strategy to the next level, to implementation. You will need to take the conceptual problem and create a concrete solution using IT tools and techniques. This will be the case whether the problem is creating a new accounting system to complement the new chart of accounts created by the accountants or a new product that will allow the company to grab significant market share from your chief competitor. You will need to adopt the personality of a tactician. You will need to make things happen.

Do you remember our earlier discussion about application languages? Well, this discussion will be very similar in that there are a number of development methodologies that you could use to create the proper IT solutions. There are also a number of techniques for developing tactical plans. These plans are sometimes called action plans. Whatever the name, these plans will convert the strategic plans into step-by-step tasks that will fulfill the strategic direction.

Remember that all the CIO's plans will not be restricted to the IT department. While some technical endeavors, such as upgrading data center equipment, may only include IT areas, most tasks will impact other business units and will need to integrate with the business unit plans. Whichever tactical planning technique(s) you adopt, your plan should have the flexibility to include non-IT business areas.

When developing action plans, it is important to remember that multiple projects will be established as a result of those plans. All of these projects, like the plans themselves, will need to be integrated and coordinated. Some of the projects will be within the IT department while others will be in the other business units. They will all need to be managed together to effectively implement the strategy. We will discuss this idea in more depth in the section entitled "CIO the Program Manager."

Suffice it to say that the CIO Tactician personality is extremely important to the success of the company's strategic endeavors.

CIO the Business Partner

As CIO, if you think that you are the only person who cares about IT, think again. Think of all the executives in your company. About 20 percent of their time is spent thinking about your organization and the things that your organization does every day. Now add the time that *you* spend on the same subject. That's a lot of concern about one facet of the company's operations. When you deal with your executive peers, it is important that your business partner personality is aware of this.

IT matters to companies regardless of some of the current writings to the contrary. Not only does it matter, it is a critical component to the corporate strategy. Information technology is used to cut costs, develop new products, manage the corporate assets, and a whole host of other things that help the company gain a competitive advantage. As a result, your executives are going to think about it a lot.

You may be asking, "How does that affect my business partner personality?" Good question.

It will be your job to be a good business partner when it comes to what your executive colleagues are thinking about. You need to understand what concerns them most and assure them that your IT organization's goals, objectives, and strategy are focused on those thoughts and concerns. Someone once said that "We have two ears and only one mouth for a reason." Feeling that most of the corporation is trying to run your organization is a natural tendency. Sometimes the feeling may even be justified. But this personality should exercise the use of two ears. The thoughts that your business partners are having about IT will more than likely be thoughts about moving the enterprise forward…or about driving the competition crazy…or about reducing costs…or about…I think you get the idea.

> **What advice would you give a new CIO that had just been placed in the position?**
>
> *"I would say that an incumbent CIO needs to get to know the whole company as intimately as possible. Good relations with the CFO and financial department are equally as important as good relations with the CEO. Since most companies aren't too familiar with their IT department, it is imperative that the incumbent CIO is able to articulate the technological needs so that unanimous approval translates into a realistic budget, which improves the company's IT functions seamlessly. This, in turn, ultimately translates into a good company image (one that is making sound decisions), and ultimately, into cost-effective, profit-making decisions."*
>
> Suzanne Tonini, CIO
> MTR, Inc.

You may have noticed that I used the terms *business partner, peers,* or *executive colleagues* to describe the internal people who are concerned about IT. You did not see me use terms such as, *customer* or *internal customer.* That was intentional. In my opinion, the *only* customers are the ones paying the checks to the enterprise. I know that may sound a little stringent, but I need you to tolerate my narrow-mindedness for a minute. If we work with my definition of customer, then *all* of the executives in the company are working to satisfy that *customer* so that the checks keep coming. That means that instead of a group of management people trying to serve each other (i.e., the concept of internal customers), the attention of the management is on the external customer. This transforms a group of people into a team whose primary focus is to work as business partners to satisfy the *real* customer.

This concept is very important to you as CIO. You want to provide the best service that you possibly can to the people who send checks to your company…and you should. On the flip side, your business partners want you to provide *them* with the best service that you possibly can. The fact that you are providing a service to them could quickly categorize you as a service provider, and they become the customers of that service. The danger here is that you are viewed like any other vendor and not as a true member of the company's management team, whose objective is to satisfy the real customer. Some might argue that you should treat vendors as business partners as well. I agree with this concept. Yet there will always be a psychological distance between you and a vendor. This distance could also be created between you and your business partners when you treat them as customers. If that were to happen, do you think you could truly be thought of as a part of the team? Maybe, maybe not. In any case, your business partner personality should be aware of this potential problem.

CIO the Financial Manager

The global investment in information technology (including telecommunications) totaled $1.9 trillion in 2003. In addition, IT spending on a global basis was expected to climb to $2.0 trillion in 2004. At the time of this writing, over $300 billion is being spent in the United States on computers, communications equipment, networks, work group computing, and desktop/laptop computers annually. The average annual IT budget in U.S. companies is about $85 million and growing. In order for you to be successful as a CIO, it is imperative you realize that your financial manager personality is a considerable part of your CIO persona.

As a result of major scandals exposing corporate fraud and corruption, your financial manager personality is taking on a stronger role. At one time, this personality was only concerned about whether or not the IT investment yielded the appropriate return on investment (ROI). That is still an extremely important aspect of this personality. Yet Senator Paul Sarbanes and Representative Michael Oxley have forever altered the scope of this personality.

The Sarbanes-Oxley Act was signed into law on July 30, 2002, and introduced highly significant legislative changes to financial practice and corporate governance regulation. It introduced stringent new rules with the stated objective "to protect investors by improving the accuracy and reliability of corporate disclosures made pursuant to the securities laws."

Senator Sarbanes and Representative Oxley were the architects of the namesake legislation. The creation of the act followed a series of high-profile scandals, such as Enron, Tyco, and WorldCom. The President of the United States highlighted the intention of the legislation when he said that it was passed to "deter and punish corporate and accounting fraud and corruption, ensure justice for wrongdoers, and protect the interests of workers and shareholders." This high-profile legislation has significant impacted every company, since reporting compliance is mandatory. This has significant implications not only to your company, but also to you, the CIO. In addition to requiring personal attestations from the CEO and CFO as to the accuracy of the financial reports, the legislation has stringent reporting rules both on content and timing. You need to be concerned about the operation of any application system that affects the company's ability to comply with this legislation.

As previously mentioned, you also need to be cognizant of the company's ROI on its IT investment. It will be your job to ensure that the company is receiving the appropriate value for that investment. You must concern yourself with where the information technology dollars are being spent. You will need to ask the following questions:

1 "Is this the appropriate technology for this company?"

2 "Is now the time to invest in this technology?"

3 "Are these purchases consistent with the corporate strategy?"

4 "Are these expenditures consistent with the technology strategy (which should be integrated with the business strategy)?

5 "What is the worst possible thing that could happen if we did not make the purchase at this time?"

Your financial manager personality is the custodian of the finances under your auspices. Sometimes you will be the custodian of finances that are *not* under your auspices. For example, as CIO you will more than likely be responsible for *all* computer and information technology purchases. You must exercise the same fiduciary responsibilities as if the purchases were made by your department. In other words, ask the same questions. I assure you, it will not make you popular, but it will ensure that the value that your company and its shareholders are receiving is consistent with the IT investment.

CIO the Intrapreneur

One of the most exciting things about being an entrepreneur is the constant flow of creativity and innovation. An entrepreneur endlessly develops new ideas to make them look better, feel better, and improve their productivity. I have always wondered, "Where do good entrepreneurs come from?"

In 1985, Gifford Pinchot III wrote a book entitled *Intrapreneuring*. In it he talks primarily about the brain drain that takes place in organizations. Brain drain occurs when companies ignore innovative ideas. They allow their creative people to leave the company and implement their ideas as entrepreneurs, thereby draining the company of good brainpower (Pinchot, 1985). So the answer to the question, "Where do good entrepreneurs come from?" is simple; we create them in our companies and then force them to leave. Mr. Pinchot suggests that we become intrapreneurs. We must become entrepreneurial without leaving our company.

I think that as CIOs, we not only have to have an intrapreneur personality, we also have to create an intrapreneurial IT environment. We must create an environment for creativity and innovation to flourish. A good definition of the acronym CIO is "Chief Innovation Officer," because a key part of your job is just that…innovation.

Let's talk a little bit more about innovation. Peter Drucker once said, "Business has only two functions—marketing and innovation." The intrapreneur has to make innovation a hygiene factor in their organization. Let me explain what I mean by hygiene factor. There are things that we automatically do as normal human beings to maintain good hygiene. For example, we don't think about brushing our teeth in the morning, we just do it. We don't think about taking a shower each day, we just do it. We don't think about combing our hair or putting on clean clothes, we just do it. In the same way, your organization should not have to think about whether it will be innovative. It should just be something you do.

As chief intrapreneur, your job is to convert technological innovation into exceptional business opportunities for your company. You need to turn your organization into an idea-generating machine. To create an innovative organization, you must first understand that the creative mind does not reside in a particular level within your department. People at every level can be innovative. Creating the innovation a company needs to move to the next level requires a focused effort on harnessing and releasing human potential and creativity, regardless of its origin. That does not mean that everyone will be good at creating ideas. Some people will be really good at coming up with ideas, and some will be really good at implementing them. You will need both. Encouraging innovation does not mean that you must pursue or even like every idea that is generated. First you must acknowledge the intent and risk of the idea, then address any possible issues that may arise as a result, and, finally, if appropriate, implement it.

Many executives believe that technology carries the promise of tomorrow. It is the job of your intrapreneur personality to fulfill that promise. Your investment in innovation will create your company's future, because it is the lifeblood of all growing organizations. You must have a constant commitment to innovation and the creation of new ideas. It should be a passion for you and your organization.

Yet innovation does not always mean you must start from scratch. Sometimes it is a matter of taking something that currently exists and looking at it in a different way. Usually, the underlying technology was already in existence. You must also keep in mind that, like the business strategy, your innovation must integrate with the business innovation to unleash the company's maximum potential.

Finally, you must not fall into the trap of accepting a creative idea as the panacea to all your company's future problems. Be aware that today's incredible innovation will be tomorrow's expected way of doing business. Remember, innovation must be a hygiene factor in your organization.

CIO the Program Manager

As CIO, your program manager personality will frequently become the most dominant personality. There will always be a large number of integrated projects that will need to be managed simultaneously. Let's get a better understanding of this personality and the components that will help it to become successful.

An air traffic controller at a busy airport manages the position, altitude, speed, and location of all the aircraft under their auspices. A juggler is cognizant of the height, weight, and speed at which the objects being juggled are falling. A pharmacist is always extremely accurate in the dosages of many different drugs. In addition, they understand how all of those drugs interact with each other. A wing commander knows, understands, and manages the precise position, speed, altitude, and location of every aircraft in the precision flying team. To prevent a disaster, each professional must have an exact understanding of the many activities over which he or she has control. Some of the control is direct, some indirect. None of these people have the luxury of daydreaming. The air traffic controller, pharmacist, or wing commander can *never* have an off day. Of course, depending on the items being juggled, knives, for instance, this also holds true for the juggler. You will feel like each of these individuals when you perform the functions under your program manager personality.

Let's examine the differences between a *project* and a *program* so that you can better understand the functions of the program manager persona. A project is a specific activity with a well-defined, predetermined result. It has a discrete beginning and end. Since a project is a specific activity, it is different from all of the other projects and will produce a one-of-a-kind artifact. A project may be established to develop a new accounting system, create a new pricing structure, or reengineer a business process.

A program, on the other hand, is a collection of integrated projects. The projects are managed collectively as one overall effort. There will be interdependencies between the projects, even though the projects themselves are independent. The duration of a program begins with the start of the first project within the program and ends with the completion of the last project. A program will include projects from many different divisions and/or departments within the company. In many instances, other companies will also have plans in the program. This is especially true of programs that include vendor companies or customers from other companies. As a result, programs tend to have a senior-level governance structure. A new product launch would be an example of a program. Let's see why this is so.

The launching of a new product requires the activities from virtually every department in the company. The product development department converts the prototype into the final design of the product. Manufacturing determines the tools necessary to make the product. Marketing understands and targets those who will buy the product and all of the demographics associated with the market. Finance determines the price of the product so that a profit can be achieved. Information technologies designs and develops the supporting application systems. For some products (e.g., insurance products), the systems are the products. Sales develops the techniques that will influence customers to purchase the product. Distribution warehouses the product and determines the best method for getting it into the hands of the customer. Human resources (HR) determines if the company has the skills necessary to develop and launch the product. Whether the skills exist within the company or not, HR has to have a project established to acquire the necessary people and the skills. In addition, they develop both the internal and external training needed. Senior management determines the strategic timing of announcements, communication, and the new product launch, as well as approves all stages of development.

Each business unit develops a project or a series of projects to accomplish their respective responsibilities in the new product launch. Yet a number of interdependencies exist across projects, as well as across departments. For example, it will be difficult for marketing to determine the demographics or for manufacturing to decide the necessary machine tooling before product development has completed designing the product. Likewise, it will be tough for the finance department to determine a price without understanding the market in which it will be sold. There are many other scenarios that I could provide, but I think you get the idea.

Some of the following questions arise in a program such as this one:

- Who is responsible for overseeing all of the interdependencies between all of the projects and all of the departments?
- Who communicates the status of the overall product launch to senior management?
- Who determines the impact of a slippage in one of the projects on the overall product launch program?
- Who decides which projects have priority when a conflict arises?
- What common rules will all of the projects follow, regardless of department?
- How are changes in priorities, goals, direction, or target dates effectively communicated to all of the projects that are underway within each department?

There are many, many more questions that you will probably encounter during a program such as a new product launch. But at this point your question is probably, "Why is this important to the CIO?"

In many, many companies, the most experienced project managers are in the information technology department. These project managers generally have experience on all size projects. Usually, they have experience in managing multiple projects simultaneously. In addition, IT usually has the most disciplined project management processes. It is only natural that senior management—looking for an area to manage the new launch program—will assign it to the CIO. That's you.

When the program is assigned to you (and I assure you, one will be), the first thing that you must do is establish a governance and management structure that will be followed by all projects under the program. This governance will begin with the establishment of a program management office and program management structure. The program management office is responsible for guiding the entire program through all phases by doing the following:

- Tracking and communicating program-wide progress based on the collective project plans of every project in the program.
- Managing the program budget.
- Developing and monitoring change management processes.
- Developing and monitoring issue management processes.

The program management structure will include both a management review board (usually chaired by the president or CEO) and a steering committee (usually made up of the heads of every department). Roles and responsibilities as well as decision-making authority must be defined for all levels within the program management structure. A process will need to be established for how communication will take place within and between the projects, between the departments, and to senior management. This will include how the project status is developed and reported.

You need to develop a change management process. A change is an activity that alters functionality, deliverables, the budget, any interfaces, or any dates. Change management is a method to record, track, and manage all changes across the program. This process will define how changes are reported, to whom they are reported, how often they are reported, and who has authority to approve the change. Some changes will exist solely at the project level; some will exist at the program level; and some at both levels. Regardless, the method for reporting and resolving changes needs to be the consistent at all levels. The following is an example of a change process model:

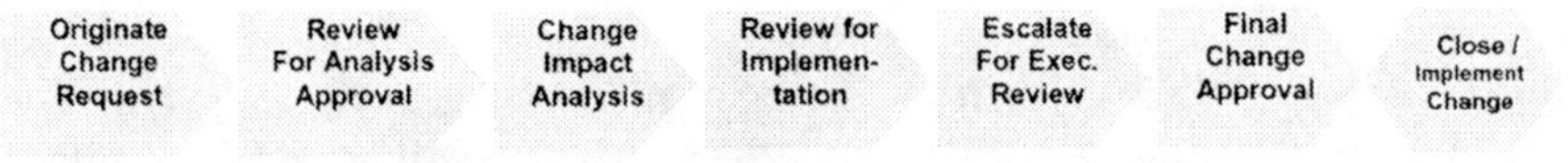

| Originate Change Request | Review For Analysis Approval | Change Impact Analysis | Review for Implemen-tation | Escalate For Exec. Review | Final Change Approval | Close / Implement Change |

Figure 5. Example of change process model.

You must also develop and implement an issue management process. An issue is a question, concern, or request regarding any aspect of the program. Issue management is the method to document, prioritize, monitor, and facilitate the resolution of issues. Here is an example of an issue process model:

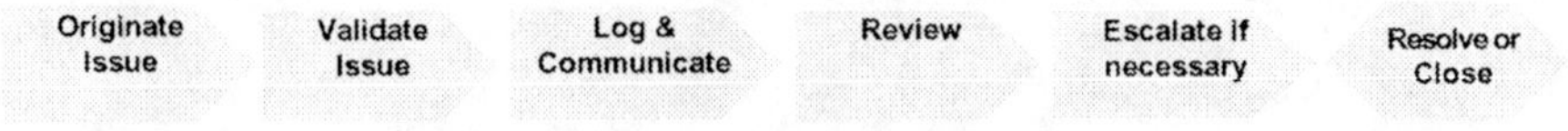

| Originate Issue | Validate Issue | Log & Communicate | Review | Escalate if necessary | Resolve or Close |

Figure 6. Example of issue process model.

The program governance will also include the management, communication, and interaction with any vendors that may be involved in the program. It will also outline the responsibilities of the vendor in the program. It will be prudent to have a senior vendor manager on one of the management committees. They may not be required to participate in every senior management meeting, but it will be crucial to have that senior level connection if a project in the vendor company has the ability to seriously impact the success of the program. This also holds true for any customer project(s) that may be participating in the program.

Even if you are not assigned the corporate level program, this information is important. You will find yourself, on many occasions, managing multiple, interdependent IT projects that will look a lot like a program. The only difference is that these projects will be confined within the IT department. In any case, you should still establish all of the disciplines of a program within your IT department.

As you can see, the program manager personality can be critical to the success of your company's strategy implementation or your specific department. Depending on the type of company you are in and the products that are produced, your success could be as critical as the air traffic controller and the wing commander. And from the company's point of view, a failure could be just as disastrous.

CIO the Economist

Today, a CIO is constantly being asked to do more with the IT department for less. In addition to increasing the productivity of the IT department, the CIO must increase the productivity of the other departments within the company as well. There is typically an expectation that this will be done through the intelligent use of technology.

Let's make sure we understand the requirement. You must be able to learn, select, and intelligently employ information technology to significantly increase the productivity of most of the departments within the company while reducing the number of technologists that you need to achieve that endeavor.

You got it.

By the way, when you are finished (or more realistically, in your spare time), you can eliminate the national debt! At the time of this writing, the national debt is about $8 trillion and growing at the meager rate of $1.63 billion a day.

I know you must be thinking that eliminating the national debt has to be much easier than implementing the productivity improvements that your company is asking you to do. But the task is not as daunting as it sounds. In the past I have used the IT department as the test bed for my productivity strategies with a great deal of success. I would test the strategy, review the portions of the strategy that failed, modify the strategy, and then retest the modified strategy. Then, after a great deal of trial and error, I would hone and implement only those productivity strategies that really worked. I use to call this my non-trivial, non-critical approach. It is non-trivial because implementing a successful strategy would increase the productivity of the IT department. It is non-critical because, if the strategy didn't work, a major business unit was not disrupted.

Oftentimes those strategies resulted in a reduction in the number of people needed in the IT department. For instance, we determined that a large amount of the programming work could be outsourced overseas (there is more information on this topic in Chapter 4 in the section entitled "To Outsource, or Not to Outsource—Not a Real Question"). Essentially this meant that a highly efficient outsourcing company could do the same work with less people at a cost significantly lower than our cost. This also freed up our highly technical people so that they could concentrate on investigating, selecting, and implementing new, productivity-increasing technologies for the company. As a result, we were able to do more with less. My team and I, working with our business partners in other business units, would develop plans for implementing the appropriate IT strategies (i.e., the ones that completed our test/fail/retest cycle) in other departments. In most cases, the strategy had to be adapted to the specific department, but the spirit of the strategy, as well as the ultimate outcome, was the same.

Your economist personality will have a major impact on the operational efficiency of the company.

CIO the Marketing Manager

> *"Business has only two functions—marketing and innovation."*
> —Peter Drucker

The marketing manager personality is a dual personality. Your first marketing personality has to be concerned internally with making sure that your business partners know and understand the services that your IT organization provides. Your other marketing personality has to determine how to support your company's marketing strategy using information technology.

The CIO position is probably one of the least understood C-level positions in the company in all of the aspects of the job. Yes, everyone understands that IT writes programs, develops systems, runs computers, and does something with databases. As you know (or at least will know by the time you finish reading this book) that there is a lot more to the CIO position. The services that you provide can help virtually every aspect of the business—from business analysis and reengineering to innovative marketing techniques using technology. You should not assume that all of your business partners know all of the ways that your department can support the efforts of their respective departments. You will have to educate them about your products and services.

The key to any marketing strategy is to understand the needs of the people who use your products and services. You need to understand the needs of your internal business partners. The only way for you to do that is to be closely involved in the planning and strategy development of their business operations. Today there are very few areas of the company that can exist without some aspect of information technology. Actually, I can't really think of any area. If an area is not using technology, then it is probably doing things manually. You will have the opportunity to do a business reengineering study that could result in an automated solution that will increase productivity. The ultimate result will be a positive impact to the bottom line of the company. Keep in mind that you would not even know that this situation existed if you were not closely aligned with or did not understand the operations of your peer's business.

At first glance, this may not seem like a difficult task. That is where your marketing personality comes in to play. Why? Although it may be blatantly obvious to you that you can provide a service, it may not be so obvious to your peers. Again, they don't understand all of the services that you have to offer, for example, as I mentioned earlier, Business Process Reengineering. What if you have a business partner who is not getting the optimum production from one of their business units? As an internal consultant you can offer this service to analyze their business processes and recommend solutions. Keep in mind that many of your systems analysts understand and perform these techniques on a regular basis when they participate in a systems development project.

You may also have a business area that recognizes it needs some automation in a certain department. It is very common for the business unit to pursue the purchase of this software outside the IT organization. This is a result of the increased independence that business units are given in order for them to produce more with less. I wouldn't be surprised if this scenario exists within your company. How does that make you feel? Angry? Left out? Like they don't feel you can support them? Rid yourself of those feelings and accept it as reality and not a criticism of your ability to perform. I also suggest that, because you and your department are skilled at creating and analyzing RFPs (requests for proposal) and selecting vendors, you offer your services to help them accomplish this task. The result should be a win-win situation and very positive for your company. You will win by keeping your finger on the technology *pulse* of the company. Your peers will win by having experienced professionals help them purchase the technology. They should be able to save money because they didn't have to purchase the expertise from outside. They would also reduce the risk of making a potentially costly purchasing mistake.

Regardless of the situation, it will take your marketing personality to internally market the efforts of your IT organization. Remember, these are just a couple of examples that I selected for illustration purposes. I am sure you can find many, many more as you think through all of the aspects of your IT organization.

Your company has a marketing philosophy, a marketing strategy, and a marketing plan. Many aspects of that strategy will require that your marketing persona be directly involved. There are basically five parts to any marketing plan. They include the following:

1   Identify your customer's needs.
2   Design and create products and services to meet those needs.
3   Communicate to your prospective customers the information about your products and services.
4   Make those products and services available to customers.
5   Price them in a way that the customer will buy them and the company will make a profit.

Most marketing texts will call these the 4 P's: product, price, place, and promotion. It will be the job of your marketing personality to understand how you can use information technology to support your company's marketing strategy. This could include everything from the online databases available for market analysis and segmentation to the use of the Web for both e-commerce and delivery.

In summary, you have the ability to have a significant impact on the success of your company. First, impact it internally by marketing the services that you have available that can help your peers succeed in their endeavors. In addition, you can use information technology to support your company's marketing philosophy, strategy, and plans. Your marketing personality must keep its eyes open for opportunities to provide a unique service to your company.

CIO the Salesperson

You are very excited…Why?

Before we answer the question *why*, we must first understand that there are different forms of excitement. There is the excitement a person feels when an attractive person enters the room. There is also the excitement a person feels when they accidentally fall off of a mountain.

Let's get back to why you are excited. It all started with a meeting you had about six months ago with the company president. He told you how the competition was gaining ground with a new product they had just developed. You listened intently. After about an hour, you told him that you would like to think about the problem because you were sure that your dynamic IT team could come up with something to help. Subsequently, you meet with some of your business partners in sales, product development, and marketing. You are sure that you have a clear picture of the problem.

You get together with your chief technology wizard and a few of your trusted designers and come up with a brilliant technology solution in less than a week. You meet with the president again to present the solution. You convince him that by implementing a modification to the current systems the company can flood the marketplace with their premier product. You explain how this solution will drive the competition crazy and secure the company's leadership in the marketplace. He likes it. He has only one question: "How long will it take to develop and implement?" You say, "Six months tops." He says, "Go for it!"

Now, here you are, six months later. You have completed the system modifications on time…and they work. You have not spent a nickel more than you predicted. You are excited.

What a salesperson. You listened to the problem, conferred with your colleagues, engineered a brilliant solution, and *sold* the president…What a salesperson!

This is the end of story, right?

Nope.

You see, another two months have passed and the *brilliant* solution has still not been implemented. You did not realize that modifications to the software systems also required modifications to the business processes of the marketing, sales, product development, and production departments. These are changes to the business processes that your colleagues are not willing to make. How can that be? They bought into—and even liked—your solution to the problem (or so you thought). They supported the decision to move forward with the system modifications. The problem was that neither you nor your business partners understood how closely connected the software systems were to the internal business processes. The processes that have worked for so long…the processes upon which your business partners' current successes are built. This new change will disrupt all that.

Another month goes by, the solution is still not implemented, and the competition is driving your company crazy!

What type of excitement are you feeling? Are you feeling the attractive person excitement or the falling off a mountain excitement?

What really happened?

Simply put, you failed to close the sale. You fell into a series of traps that nascent salespeople (and most CIOs) fall into every day. There are always a number of questions that salespeople must ask themselves before the sale is closed. Here are a few of those questions:

1 Who is the true prospect?
2 Does the prospect have a need for my product?
3 Does the prospect have the authority to buy my product?
4 Will my product help the prospect do their job better?
5 Can my prospect afford my product?
6 Did I close the sale?
7 Did I get a commitment to buy?

I understand that you are not trained to be a salesperson. You must realize, however, that these are the questions you must ask yourself about any project that you will be implementing.

It is essential that your sales personality understand it is imperative to get a complete buy-in from your internal business partners when you want to implement any project or idea. They are generally the true prospects. You need to get a commitment from them. The president or CEO will have the authority to approve your actions going forward, but it is your business partners who will have to live with the final product that you implement. It is your business partners who will have to modify the way they do business to accommodate the new system or process. You will always be affecting another department with what you do. It is vital that you close the sale with the other departments to ensure success at implementation.

CIO the Negotiator

Chief information officers in corporations do not produce anything for themselves or their IT departments. Everything that is produced by them is for the use, service, or production of some other area. You will not produce products that you will sell. CIOs do not generally design systems that are for the sole use of the IT department. You will manage projects that support the work of all of the other departments within the company. Therefore, acquiring equipment, people, money, and any other asset you need to do your job will require interacting with someone else. So, by default, virtually everything that a CIO does requires some level of negotiation. This makes the negotiator personality an extremely important characteristic of the CIO persona.

This is an attribute of the CIO position that is often overlooked by many CIOs. They never really think they need this skill. But when the functions of a CIO are analyzed—regardless of the position they hold within the company—it becomes clear that they cannot escape this skill. Many CIOs poorly demonstrate this ability because they don't think of it as a part of their repertoire of talents. Nothing could be further from the truth.

You will also be responsible for the acquisition of computer and networking equipment, for many companies, millions of dollars worth. You would never buy a car for the price on the sticker. The same is true for buying computers. The size of your company and your position within it (i.e., your buying power) will contribute to the leverage that you will have with equipment vendors. The size of your equipment budget will also play a role. These attributes do not guarantee discounts, reduced prices, or preferred rates. Like everything else, they will need to be negotiated.

The *American Heritage* dictionary defines the word *negotiate*: "To confer with another or others in order to come to terms or reach an agreement." The key word in this definition is *agreement*. In other words, to negotiate is to make an arrangement between you and the other parties regarding some course of action, some amount of money, some number of people, some amount of equipment, or some other item you need to produce the requested product. If your company's department heads are asking for the product, why is it necessary to negotiate for the resources required to produce the requested product? This seems like a straightforward and logical question. Therefore, the answer should also be straightforward and simple, right?

Well, not really.

There are a variety of reasons why acquiring the resources to do your job may be a lot more difficult than you anticipated. For example, your company may have a policy to only spend *x*% of the expected revenue dollars on IT expenditures. Those dollars are then allocated to the various departments using some unique internal formula. The IT work that the departments need to accomplish their respective goals is more than the amounts that they have been allocated. As a result, the departments have one of two choices. Either take the money from some other line item within their budgets or *negotiate* with the CIO to get more than their budgets can afford. It has been my experience that they will generally take the negotiation route. In order for them to succeed in that endeavor and complete the negotiation, you have to *agree*.

You must be asking yourself, "How can I possibly agree to complete a project with less than the required resources necessary to be successful?" Unfortunately, for what ever reasons, CIOs do it every day. They embark on projects doomed from the start because of lack of resources rather than negotiate a more achievable agreement. A negotiation could result in a reduced scope. In addition, the negotiation could implement a phased approach that will extend the project over multiple budget periods. Regardless of the negotiation, the end result should be an increased probability of success.

As a company senior manager, you will participate in the same budget process as your business partners that will allocate your spending amounts as well. You will look at the amount of project requests that you have received from the other departments, the skills that you need to acquire to complete those projects, the new and upgraded equipment that will be necessary, and many other things that will be necessary for you to be successful. You will then look at your initial allocation and become painfully aware of the significant disparity in what you need and what you were allocated. In many instances, based on the strategic nature of the projects, you will be able to negotiate a larger allocation. Be prepared for that negotiation to be difficult. You will be competing with all of the other expenditures that many within your company consider necessary to produce "real" products and services. They may not consider your department's products and services 'real' because they don't really understand the nature of what you do. A prelude to any negotiation should be an understanding of the impact on the company or department of *not* having the required resources. For example, when asking for new equipment, people unfamiliar with IT may think you are just trying to purchase the latest and greatest technology. It will be your job to ensure that they understand the increased number of transactions that can be processed (and the increased revenue or productivity), or the extra security that will prevent a serious breach, or the reduced downtime, or whatever business impact would result.

Your negotiations do not end with the budget cycle. You need to negotiate with vendors for the equipment (see "CIO the Vendor Manager"), negotiate with the finance and human resource departments for the resources that you need, and, of course, you need to negotiate with your people. What? What do you mean negotiate with my people? Unless you are in a company that always gives you the amount that you need when you need it—don't laugh; I think there are a couple of companies on the planet like that—your people will believe you have lost your mind. They will be convinced that there is no way they can produce what you are asking with the resources allocated. You will essentially have to negotiate with your people about getting the work done successfully.

It is difficult to cover all aspects of the CIO negotiator personality without writing a book within a book. Therefore, I hope you agree that the aforementioned topic gives you enough to understand the importance of you developing this skill. If so, then I have been successful in this negotiation. You see, you even have to negotiate with me!

CIO the Motivationalist

It has been said many times that you can't motivate people. Does that mean that an objective to motivate people is an unattainable task? Or is it simply an impossible paradox? Regardless of this dilemma, as a senior manager, you are well aware that being a motivationalist is a requirement of your position.

How can that be?

If we assume that it is possible to motivate people, then the real problem is that the senior management team generally has no idea how to motivate information technology professionals. This is because they do not know how to speak in "bits, bytes, and real-time." As you may have guessed, they have no desire to learn how to speak in the obscure language of the information systems professional. After all, that is why they hired you. They assume you not only know how to speak that language but have a desire to do so. Senior management thinks that if you know how to communicate with IT professionals, you know how to motivate them to fulfill the corporate strategy.

As a manager, it is imperative that you get your team of professionals to perform tasks and complete significant units of work. Work that, for a variety of reasons, they would not normally do on their own. Work that is not only a requirement for them to finish, but work that must be completed correctly and within the established timeframe and quality levels. Work that is important to accomplishing the goals of the company.

How do you do that if people cannot be motivated?

I once heard a quote: "The hardest part of politics is pleasing the voter without giving them what they want." Most of us believe that the politicians are pretty successful at it too. The question is, "How do they do that and still get us to vote for them?" More importantly, "How are they so successful at it?"

Why is it that we can sit and watch an amusing beer commercial and then get up and go to the refrigerator and get a cold one without thinking about it? Why is it possible for us to see a hamburger commercial and then feel this overwhelming need to sink our teeth into a Big Mac? How do the advertisers, motivational researchers, and psychologists get us to perform acts whether we want to or not? If they are using tricks, can you use those same tricks to motivate your systems people?

"When a systems person looks like they are about to swim, throw them a bag of rocks." I established this motivational technique many years ago, and it always seemed to work for me. One thing that system professionals seem to have in common is that they all like a challenge. Whether the challenge is a sticky technical problem or a particularly complex crossword puzzle, they derive a great deal of energy and personal pleasure from its resolution. A technique that I have used in the past is to frame the corporate objectives and goals as a problem that could only be solved by the analytical skills of the systems professionals. I would outline it as a problem that needed some technology that did not then exist or some procedure that had not been invented as yet. I was always amazed at how often they would come up with creative and innovative solutions that helped move the company forward.

WIIFM…I have always looked at this as the most important radio station on the planet. It is the station within most of the workers in our society today. It is the station whose call letters are the basis for us to get people to do whatever we need them to do. "What's In It For Me?" Is this a real radio station? No. Are the call letters really a key to get people to do things for you? Absolutely. You must understand that there is always some internal reason why someone does what you want them to do. They derive some benefit from the completion of the task. That benefit may or may not be monetary. Bob Nelson makes that point very clear in his book *1001 Ways to Reward Employees.* Sometimes, rather then giving a monetary reward, the incentive could simply be the satisfaction of knowing that they were the ones who accomplished the task. It is imperative that you learn the benefit that your people like. For some, it will be knowledge; others, the sense of accomplishment; and still others, the potential for advancement. Discovering your employees' incentive will be the key to getting them to accomplish whatever it is you need them to accomplish, and it will help your motivationalist personality to succeed.

CIO the Vendor Manager

As the CIO, you will buy computers, networks, databases, software, equipment, training, people, skills, and a whole host of other things. In addition, you may outsource some or all of your services to a specialty company. You may have to manage a large project that requires outside consultants with a particular expertise that you lack. You will need software tools to increase the productivity of your professional staff. If a physical building is a part of your organization, you will need electricians, heating and cooling people, janitors, and others to maintain that structure. This means that you will need to research, acquire, negotiate contracts, and select and manage vendors.

Your vendor manager personality will be one of the toughest personalities you will have. There are many decisions tied directly to the behavior of this persona. As vendor manager, you will need to ensure that your pursuit of outside services is tied to your company and IT strategic direction. You will find a plethora of technology and equipment that people want you to buy. Some of it may even work in your company. That technology will only be valuable to your company if it progresses the strategic direction. Otherwise, it's just another toy for the technicians.

You will have to execute a procedure for narrowing the field of players in the vendor pool to acquire the services that you need. Using a request for information or RFI process is useful when you are pursuing services about which you know little. In other words, you don't know what you don't know. This process gives the vendors very general (and sometimes sketchy) information about what you need and requests they send you information about their products or services. This can help you clarify what is available. You can then send out a more-detailed request for proposal or RFP to the specific companies that have products and services closely aligned with your needs.

Using the RFP process will narrow the number of vendors to just a select few. At this point, your toughest negotiator personality (see "CIO the Negotiator") will take over. Ensure that the vendor's company has a style and a culture that will fit within your company. Remember, most vendor relationships will continue over a long period of time. It is imperative that the vendor company fit your company's style. All of the points that were presented to you by the salesperson need to be written in the contract. If there are multiple versions of the contract during the negotiation period, make sure that none of the previously negotiated terms *fall out* of the ensuing versions.

You will need to be aware of a great many ploys during the contract negotiations. Many times a vendor will pull a bait and switch with the personnel assigned to the project. A vendor will provide you with highly skilled people at the beginning of the project and then promptly move them off to another contract after the project gets underway. This will leave your project with less-qualified people, which could jeopardize its success. Make sure that your contract documents the skills of the key people assigned to you and guarantees that they remain on the project for its duration.

The key negotiation is the price of the product or service for which you will be paying. There are numerous books, tapes, and courses on negotiation techniques that you can use to hone these skills. (I have previously mentioned the importance of these skills. See "CIO the Negotiator.") Gather all the quotes from your selected vendor list before you begin negotiations. You will want to make sure that each of the vendors on your short list knows they are competing against other vendors for your business.

You will need to make a decision as to whether the vendor will work offsite or at your location. Most people will generally recommend the vendor be located onsite with your team. This is especially important if the vendor is located a great distance from your company (e.g., you are in Chicago, and the vendor is located in San Francisco). It is generally easier to manage their activities when they are onsite. It also reduces integration problems as the project develops.

You may consider establishing a vendor management office (VMO) within your organization. The VMO would be staffed with people skilled in negotiations, contract management, and finance. The rules for how your vendors will interact with your VMO should also be negotiated into the final contract. You will need your VMO to establish policies and procedures for how your professional team will interact with the vendors. This will help to avoid confusion and possible inadvertent violations of the contract.

Think through the type of relationship that you will have with your vendor(s). Will all of your dealings be at arm's length? Or are you willing to share your strategic direction with them? Will you treat your vendors as commodity suppliers or as strategic partners? Strategic alliances with some vendors (e.g., Microsoft, HP, etc.) could be beneficial to your overall strategic direction. A strong strategic alliance with your vendor could help you find the best solution to your endeavor. Whether or not you set up a strategic alliance with your vendor is important for understanding how the relationship will develop over time.

In summary, your vendor management personality will be busy. It is extremely rare for an IT organization to deal with only one vendor. You will often not only deal with multiple vendors, but you will work with them on an integrated project in which many different vendors are participating. It would be wishful thinking to believe that if something went wrong on a project all of the vendors would collaborate on finding a solution. The reality is that they will probably explain how the other vendor is to blame. You need to be prepared to manage this environment. The trend toward multiple-vendor environments and large outsourcing contracts means that you, as CIO, can realize a tremendous benefit from a having a vendor management office. Establishing a vendor management office could remove a number of time-consuming tasks from your to-do list.

CIO the Change Agent

"You must be the change you wish to see in the world."
—Mahatma Gandhi

Henry Ford once said, "The future ain't what it used to be." Your change agent personality will need to make this quote a reality in your company.

We constantly hear phrases like, "Change is inevitable," or "The only constant that we can expect is change." Today, with increased global competition, extremely rapid advances in technology, and the subsequent growth in customer knowledge and sophistication (partly as a result of that technology), companies must change, and change quickly. Some argue that if a company does not adopt a standard set of processes for change, it will rapidly lose any competitive advantage that it may have. Simply put, it will not be able to survive.

Existing business processes that are inefficient and cumbersome often inundate businesses and slow their progress. These processes make it impossible for the company to respond to changing market conditions. This is a problem that you will have the opportunity to solve. Your change agent personality will be required to keep you and your company focused on the company's key objectives by eliminating inefficient and unnecessary processes.

> **If you had to come up with a three-word definition for CIO instead of 'Chief Information Officer', what would it be?**
>
> *"Technology Change Agent"*
>
> *Jeffry Ziegler, CIO*
> *Protocol LMS*

People and Change

In organizations, there are many types of changes that take place that affect employees—outsourcing (which we will discuss later), downsizing (or sometimes referred to by the euphemism "rightsizing"), reorganizations or organizational transformations, changes in the company's basic business model, mergers, acquisitions, and many other events. Let's not forget about the changes that you will implement as a result of your application development, technology innovations, and projects.

Whenever we talk about change, the idea of the life cycle usually comes up. The life cycle consists of the phases that people usually go through as a result of some significant change in their lives. We talk about it when we have lost a loved one or experienced some other life-changing event. These phases have been described in as few steps as four (i.e., shock, anger, resistance, and acceptance) to as many as nine steps (i.e., apprehension, denial, anger, resentment, depression, cognitive dissonance, compliance, acceptance, and internalization) that people go through when confronted with change. The average life cycle is seven steps: shock, denial, understanding, acceptance, experimentation, rationalization, and institutionalization. Regardless of the cycle, you need to understand that attitudes toward change result from a complex interplay of emotions. These emotions are what psychologists call cognitive processes. Everyone reacts to change differently. On the positive side, change is seen by some as opportunity, rejuvenation, progress, innovation, and growth. Just as legitimately, to others change can be seen as instability, upheaval, unpredictability, threat, and disorientation. Whether people perceive change with fear, anxiety, and demoralization, with excitement and confidence, or somewhere in between depends partially on the individual's psychological makeup, partially on management's actions, and partially on the specific nature of the change that you are trying to implement.

Most executives would agree that the main reason for the failure of any change initiative is the resistance to that change. What is resistance? Resistance is any force that you encounter that slows or stops your movement or progress. The strength of that force will be directly related to how people perceive the change that you are implementing.

You must realize that you are one of the company's primary change agents.

As one of the company's change agents, you will observe a similar set of behaviors and resistance as you introduce and implement new technology, processes, procedures, and techniques into the organization. You will experience the shock, anger, denial, resistance, acceptance, experimentation, and the institutionalizing of the changes that you implement. Why? Because you are changing people's lives. You will be moving people out of their comfort zones. Most of the people in the organization have been doing things the same way for a long period of time. Their existing methods and processes are comfortable, safe, understood, and—most importantly to them—they work. The need for change, in their eyes, is neither necessary nor welcomed. By the way, the people who resist change are in good company. Even the Greek philosopher Parmenides of Elea in the fifth century BC denied the existence of change!

Then, as change agent, what should you do?

Well, don't take it personally. It is not you that they are reacting to; it is the shift from their comfort zone that really bothers them. You just happened to be the person who introduced the shift.

As change agent, you need to understand and recognize what stages of the change life cycle your people are in at any given point in time. In other words, different people will be in different stages. You must have a strategy for dealing with people, depending on the stage in which they reside. For example, if you observe that someone (or some department) is in the denial or resistance phases, you may want to educate them on the benefits of the change(s) you are introducing. This will help them move into the acceptance and experimentation phases quicker. This strategy must be an integral part of your implementation plans. It is amazing how often CIOs overlook this strategy when they are planning and executing new implementations. It is a vital component in any successful implementation.

Let's consider building change strategies for the organization.

Change Strategies

You will have to develop change strategies in order for your change to succeed. Estimate what impact your change will have on the organization's behavior patterns, work processes, technological requirements, and people. You need to assess what your people's reactions will be and design a change strategy that will provide support through the process of change. You must then implement, disseminate, monitor, and adjust the program where necessary. Your change strategy should include the following:

- Clearly describe the change process to all people involved and explain the reasons why the changes are occurring. The information should be complete, unbiased, reliable, transparent, and timely. In other words: communicate, communicate, and communicate. You should make sure that your communications strategy can handle questions during the change process.

> **As a change agent, how do you get the organization to change?**
>
> *"The first step is to build credibility by delivering solid results. A CIO I worked for used the mantra, 'Underpromise and overdeliver.' Once others know you will accomplish things that help move the organization forward, they will be more willing to listen to ideas involving change. Having key constituents involved in the decision-making (including your biggest critics) helps smooth the path. Always have sound business reasons for changes and avoid making change just for the sake of change."*
>
> **Vince Sheehan, CIO**
> **Indiana University School of Medicine**

- Effectively implement the change in alignment with organizational objectives, major environmental trends, and the perceptions and feelings of the people.

- Provide support to the people in the organization as they deal with the change.

- Involve the employees directly in the change process.

- Anticipate the possibility that some relationships may get damaged. One element of your strategy should be designed to rebuild those relationships.

- Ensure that there is a feedback mechanism to assess whether the changes are having the desired result.

There are many resources available to help you understand the change management process. It is important for you to educate yourself on these techniques. Your change agent personality will get a real workout during your tenure as CIO. If you are doing your job, you will constantly be introducing some type of change to the organization on a regular basis. Sometimes the change that you introduce will be inside your own IT department. You should understand that the reaction you receive within your internal organization will be similar (if not identical) to the reaction that you get when you introduce changes to the company. Do not restrict your change strategies to those outside your IT organization.

In summary, you need to recognize that some people will welcome change. A larger number will probably resist it. It is important to develop a change management strategy as a part of your implementation plans that will anticipate and address that resistance. When you do, your change agent persona will succeed.

CIO the Industry Expert

You are the chief of information. You are the center of the data and information assets. Your knowledge, skills, and talents are unmatched in your company. You need to keep your finger on the pulse of the industry. In your company, you *are* the industry expert. There are things that you must do to ensure that you fulfill that role successfully.

It is easy to overlook this personality. You are managing (or more appropriately, juggling) vendors, budgets, business expectations, systems professionals, strategic plans, performance statistics, security threats, and many other things. You will do all of this at the same time. Carve out time to attend conferences, participate in professional organizations, and, whenever possible, be the keynote speaker at these events.

Doing these things is an extremely inexpensive way to gain a tremendous education. You will gain access to a large number of people who, very possibly, have gone through what you are about to go through. The pool of knowledge and experience at these functions is unsurpassed. It goes up exponentially when you add the consultants, industry analysts, vendors, developers, authors, and IT business experts who also attend these events.

Consider giving speeches at these venues. This could be an extremely economical way for you to advertise your company to a large number of people. I have also found that whenever I speak at events, people are always eager to come up to me and tell me their stories. You will not believe the number of times that the solution to a sticky problem I was dealing with was buried in one of those stories.

By participating in these functions and meeting a large number of people, you can establish a large network of professionals. You can then tap into that network when you embark on a new task. Your established cadre of experts will help you avoid mistakes that they have already overcome. Use this personality whenever possible. It will prove a tremendous benefit both to you and your company.

CIO the Security Chief or CSO

Let's talk about your paranoid personality. Security is an area that is extremely important to your company and your role as the CIO. Regardless of how much you think you know about information systems security, it won't be enough. You may think you have all of the technology, skilled professionals, and infrastructure you need to protect the corporation's information assets (i.e., databases, operating systems, business applications, etc.), but there is a plethora of thieves, viruses, and network hackers dedicated to attacking your information systems. One thing my experience as a data security person taught me early in my career was that *a thief with enough time and enough resources can crack any security system that you develop.*

There is virtually no level of technology that can outwit the ingenuity of a clever dishonest person. There are literally tens of millions of virus and hacker attacks each year on corporate computers worldwide. As the CIO, you are expected to deal effectively with these threats. As the corporation's technologist, you are also the corporation's chief guardian of its data and information assets. If your responsibility includes the data centers, that could include physical assets. In addition to obvious criminal threats such as sabotage and fraud, you will also need to be concerned about inadvertent errors that could alter or damage the data asset. You will need to establish controls and procedures for monitoring, detecting, and eliminating the pressures on the assets for which you are responsible. The easy part of the information security persona is writing policies and procedures. The difficult part is getting your business partners to follow the rules you have so arduously developed. The procedures and controls you have put in place will more than likely cause them to perform additional work not directly connected to their products, services, or product development, so they will resist your procedures.

As mentioned in the previous chapter, if your responsibilities include the buildings and facilities, you may also need to secure non-IT assets. These buildings and facilities may be restricted to just the data center(s) or may include all of the brick-and-mortar assets of the enterprise. Regardless, it will be your responsibility to ensure that they are secure. A security breach could come in the form of sabotage, fire, flood, intrusion, or, sometimes, simple mistakes.

Are you thinking to yourself, "Whew, I don't have to worry much about IT security because we have an Internet firewall that is protecting us"?

Wrong.

Internet firewalls are really great for stopping about 90 percent of the network traffic violations. As firewalls with increased sophistication develop, hackers are cleverly developing more ways to tear down those walls. Hackers are finding ways through the firewalls and are attacking applications directly. The sophistication of the firewalls needs to increase to address this new type of intrusion as well as the growing intelligence of the hacker. This is just one area of security that should be in your line of sight. There are many more.

It will be your responsibility to establish a security-conscious environment where the management of risks against the corporate data asset is a standard operating procedure. Ensure that this security consciousness includes an understanding of the legal, ethical, and privacy issues of security. In summary, you will need to be chief of paranoia.

CIO the Asset Manager

Information is a corporate asset. It is an asset that you must manage through a life cycle, just like any other asset, including cash, buildings, machines, and people. You will manage most of these assets. Depending on your company's business model, you may manage all of these assets. As a result, you have an asset management personality.

An ordinary life cycle for the management of any asset looks something like this:

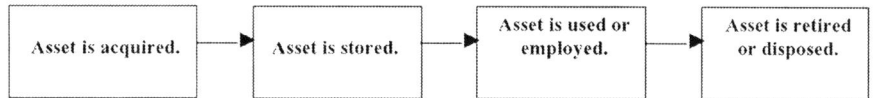

Figure 7. Generic asset management life cycle.

The information asset is as important and valuable as other corporate assets. In fact, the information asset is required to effectively manage the other corporate assets. Recognize that fact and establish a proper life cycle to manage your company's information asset. This means that you will need to develop an information life cycle management (ILM) strategy.

Let's examine the key elements of the ILM.

- Business-Focused
  IT and business needs must work together to align the key processes, applications, and business initiatives, according to the overall business strategy.

- Policy-Based
  Become familiar with government regulations such as Sarbanes-Oxley (see previous section, "CIO the Financial Manager"). Regulations mandate how long data must be retained, when it may be deleted, and who may have access to that data. It is your responsibility to establish policies for the company's information asset.

- Centrally Managed
  Provide an integrated view of all of the enterprise's information assets the same way that the CFO provides an integrated view of the money asset. You must establish central management of the company's information and data assets.

- Diverse
  Ensure that your ILM strategy can operate throughout the entire enterprise. It must encompass all the different development methods, platform types, and operating systems used in the enterprise.

- Aligned with Business Value
  Finally, you will need to ensure that you store the right information for the right period of time on the appropriate storage mechanism, consistent with the value of that information to the company. This is probably the most important aspect of your ILM strategy.

Use all of the resources under your auspices (i.e., data center, finances, people, etc.) to effectively implement your ILM strategy. For example, you will need to ensure that the information asset is secure. You will need to understand who has the authority to access and change it. You will need to know who owns it, how much there is, and where it is located. Your strategy should include how it will be made available, how it will be backed up, and, of course, how it will be recovered if it is lost, either inadvertently or through some unforeseen disaster.

This is truly one of your most important personalities. Management of the corporate assets is a basic function of every executive. Managing the information and data asset is not always as obvious as the other assets. So be prepared, you may have to invoke your salesperson personality to ensure that the company understands the value of the information asset.

Let's Sum Things Up

You will have many personalities as the chief information officer. Each professional that you deal with in your company will view a different personality and will have a different set of expectations. Often a person you encounter today will see one personality and have a particular set of expectations. Tomorrow, that same person may encounter a completely different personality. Your CEO may see you as a strategic senior manager during an offsite strategy session on one day, a financial manager during a budget session the next day, and a technology wizard during a product development meeting on the following day. As a matter of fact, they may see you as all three during the same strategy session!

You should be proud that you have these personalities. You should also be proud that you have the ability to conscientiously move freely between them. It means that you are a unique individual with abilities greater than the average professional. There are very few people on this planet that can—or even want to—do what you do. Remember, for you, having multiple personalities is normal.

Unexpected Challenges

Chapter

"In the past a leader was a boss. Today's leaders must be partners with their people...they no longer can lead solely based on positional power."

—Ken Blanchard

Any new endeavor that creates significant solutions and advancements also creates new problems and challenges. The introduction of new information technology solutions is no different. The problems and challenges that the CIO faces are very rarely of a technical nature. The challenges usually concern interactions and relationships both inside and outside of IT. Internally, people will interpret the directions of the CIO completely differently than the CIO had intended because the IT organization, by its very nature, will contain professionals with different skills, backgrounds, and objectives. Outside of IT, people expect that IT solutions *can't* go wrong. They think that if a system has issues, then that system is not valuable to the company. Of course, that is not entirely the truth.

There will be other external challenges as well, such as outsourcing, the perceptions of what the CIO does versus what the CIO really does, the level of trust that the business unit heads will have (or not have) in the CIO and the IT organization, and the general insanity that exists when people are confronted with change—any change. None of these challenges are insurmountable. A better understanding of what they are will help you manage them when you encounter them...and you will encounter them.

Let's examine some of the major challenges a little closer.

Execution Is Key

"It is an immutable law in business that words are words, explanations are explanations, promises are promises—but only performance is reality."
—Harold S. Geneen 1910–1997

Execution

  SYLLABICATION: ex·e·cu·tion

PRONUNCIATION: ĕk'sĭ·kyōō'shən

      NOUN: **1a.** The act of executing something. **b.** The state of
        being executed.
        2. The manner, style, or result of performance: *The plan
        was sound; its execution, faulty.*

You have done some interesting things since you were first made CIO. You have looked at your business processes and have identified where they need improvement; you have assessed your technological strength; you have aligned the corporation's IT direction with its business strategy and goals; and you have built and organized a dynamite team. Now you are all set, right? Now you have no choice but to be successful, right?

Wrong.

Not one of the things that you have done will mean anything if you don't deliver. To deliver, you must soundly *execute*. Execute what? Execute everything! Execute your strategies. Execute your staffing plans. Execute your project plans. Execute your relationship development strategy. Execute your technology transition plans. Execute your desktop upgrades. Execute your lunch plans! Soundly and decisively execute everything!

Execute

SYLLABICATION: ex·e·cute

PRONUNCIATION: ĕk′sĭ-kyōōt′

TRANSITIVE Inflected forms: **ex·e·cut·ed**, **ex·e·cut·ing**, **ex·e·cutes**
VERB: 1. To put into effect; carry out: *a government that executes the decisions of the ruling party.*
2. To perform; do: *execute a U-turn.*
3. To create (a work of art, for example) in accordance with a prescribed design.
4. To make valid, as by signing: *execute a deed.*
5. To perform or carry out what is required by: *execute the terms of a will.*
6. *Computer Science* To run (a program or an instruction).

In a minute we will discuss building trust at all levels. The first step to building trust is the sound execution of any objective that you have laid out. Let's talk about what that means to you.

I remember taking over an organization where the biggest complaint from my business unit partners was that my people never seemed to be on time for meetings. I looked at my own staff meetings; sure enough, I had the same problem. People were constantly coming to my meetings late as well. So I quickly determined the average salary of the people who attended my staff meetings. Then I established an average hourly rate for the people who attended that meeting…then an average minute rate (it turns out it was about $1.20 a minute). I determined that, depending on the number of people who were in the room (i.e., arrived on time), it cost the company a lot of money to have them sitting there…waiting. So I established a new rule. The rule was that for every minute a person was late to my meetings, it cost them a dollar. Not long after I established that rule (and collected a lot of money); my management staff developed a similar rule in their staff meetings. Before I knew it, my organization was complimented on consistently arriving at meetings on time! How much did we collect? That's not important. What is important is that the behavior changed, and we were perceived as an organization that delivers. What did we deliver? Change. By the way, that perception carried over to all of the subsequent projects that we managed. Interestingly enough, since we were perceived that way, the IT professionals responded to that perception by consistently delivering our projects on time. This action, of course, perpetuated how we were viewed by our business partners.

Sound execution goes beyond just getting the job done. How we execute is as important as being effective and completing what we are assigned to do. Stephen Covey states in his book *The 8th Habit, From Effectiveness to Greatness* that we must move beyond effectiveness and go all the way to greatness. This includes fulfillment, passionate execution, and significant contribution (Covey, 2004). I especially like the term "passionate execution," because that is what will set your IT organization apart from the norm. This will take your organization toward greatness. This will get your team recognized as the group that can make things happen. This is what it will take to establish the trust that will be required for success.

One final word on execution: it has to be more than a buzzword used by your team solely to appease *you*. It must be a way of life for them. You may remember my discussion about a hygiene factor (see "CIO the Intrapreneur"). There are things that we automatically do to maintain good hygiene. For example, we don't think about brushing our teeth in the morning, we just do it. Well, execution must also be a hygiene factor. Your organization should not have to think about whether it is going to soundly execute. It should just do it.

I think you understand the importance of passionate execution and the trust that it builds. I think this is a good time for us to talk a bit more about trust.

Building Trust at All Levels

It is not a secret that I spend a great deal of my time involved in community activities. I believe a corporation should strive to be a good influence in any community in which it does business. I have always endeavored to engage my company in community activities.

When dealing with community organizations, a company should establish strong relationships and trust. In many communities, this strategy is called becoming "the corporate neighbor of choice." To achieve this, a corporation has to establish a trust account that is built up over time. A company must make regular trust deposits to that account through its participation in community activities and providing financial support. Occasionally, the company may have to make trust withdrawals from the account for a variety of reasons.

You may be asking, "What does that have to do with my new job as CIO?"

It's simple. You need to understand that just because you have been appointed the new CIO does not mean that you will have the support you will need to implement your programs. That support has to be earned, usually through proving yourself trustworthy and the establishing strong relationships. That does not happen by accident. It must be a deliberate goal with a deliberate strategy. You must also establish a trust account in which you must plan to make regular deposits. Without relationships and trust, it will be extremely difficult to have a successful information office. Building trust within your company is not unlike the transformation of coal into diamonds. It is a process that involves a great deal of time and sometimes a lot of pressure.

Before we discuss a simple method for making deposits into your trust account, let's look at where you need to build the relationships and trust.

Different Levels of Deposits

You must build relationships with your information team. These are the people who will carry out the key programs and strategies that are needed to support your company. In some instances, the plans that you need to execute will not be popular. But with the right level of trust (or the right balance in your trust account), your people will execute those plans without a great deal of resistance, which could waste valuable time in a critical situation. It may seem like a no-brainer. It is not. I have seen many organizations in which the CIOs spend time building relationships with everyone except for their own team. Then, when the team is called upon to deliver a critical product, the CIO is surprised when he or she is met with resistance, challenges, and a general lack of enthusiasm. By the way, don't be fooled into thinking that resistance behaviors are always overt. Sometimes they become noticeable when projects are delayed for fairly weak reasons, unexplained rashes of illnesses, or a parade of little insurmountable problems that cause creeping delays. The team is often not totally conscious of what is happening.

When the trust account contains team member deposits, these aforementioned incidents don't seem to happen. You have probably either seen or personally worked on those teams that seem to annihilate every problem they encounter. Sustained thinking and dogged determination overcome every obstacle the team meets. As you envision that team, reflect on the leader. Think about how that team *feels* about that person. The leader probably has a great deal of team deposits in the trust account.

You need to build strong relationships and trust with your peers, your counterparts in marketing, finance, product development, human resources, the business units, and, of course, any of the technology areas not under your auspices. These are usually the other C-level people that head the aforementioned departments. These people are sometimes called your stakeholders. That is because these people are the recipients of your information work. In other words, they have a *stake* in the products that you produce. Your funding is probably based on the amount of work your counterparts are expecting you to deliver during the year. These stakeholders use the applications, products, systems, Web sites, databases, networks, and other information goods that your organization produces. Your deliverables are probably designed to make a department more efficient, to save the company money, to introduce a new product to the marketplace, to enhance an old one, to reduce the number of people necessary to perform a function, or to accomplish whatever your strategic direction dictates. Whatever the case, you will need peer deposits in your trust account to be successful and to provide the expected value. Unfortunately, like it or not, your business executives don't always trust that you are working on things that support their business strategy.

It almost goes without saying that you need to build trust with your superiors. This is usually the senior executive team (of course, if you are a member of this team then they would be your peers and the above paragraph applies). I would also include the board of directors as a part of this group. This team develops the corporate strategic direction and decides how the corporate funds will be allocated. This team will determine if you have delivered value to the corporation. These people will be the most frequent users of your multiple personalities. They will be quickly impressed by your abilities and products and easily discouraged by your lack of speed and your costs, which they don't understand. This team will only make a few deposits to your account, but these deposits will be extremely large. Keep in mind, the withdrawals could be equal to or greater than the size of the previous deposits!

You may have noticed that the people, teams, and organizations that I have mentioned have one thing in common. They are all in your corporation. They are not the only people with whom you will need to build a sturdy trust and relationship. There are also your customers who pay the bill, the vendors with whom you do business, the market analysts who determine your company's value, your competitors (yes, your competitors) with whom you may need to stand side by side with on industry issues, the community that supplies the people in your organization, your family who puts up with your crazy schedule, and your stockholders who own your company and are the ultimate beneficiaries of your efforts.

Although the deposits these people make to your trust account will not be as frequent or as significant, they cannot be overlooked.

As you can see, there are people at all levels and in all areas who can have an impact on your success. You will have to build a relationship and develop trust with all these people. Some will be through direct interactions, but others will be established through indirect means.

But then how do you get them to make deposits?

Making Deposits

There are six things you need to do to get deposits made to your trust account. These things will also build the relationships that you will need to be successful. The first three things are execute, execute, and execute. The last three things are deliver, deliver, and deliver (not necessarily in that order). Of course, I have seen a number of creative CIOs boil it down to only three activities: execute/deliver, execute/deliver, and execute/deliver. Is any part of this secret unclear? Should I repeat the magic lesson?

When I asked current CIOs the most effective technique for building relationships, 84 percent responded, "Deliver on promises." What people expect from you should be clear in your mind. You must also be clear as to what your resources can deliver. Only promise what you can deliver. Establish the plan, execute the plan, and deliver on the promise. I assure you, the positive, strong relationships will be established and the deep trust will be built. Simple to understand? Yes. Easy to do? No.

That's it.

Adding Value to the Business

You and your information office will perform a wide variety of activities. You will review technology, develop systems, manage vendors, reengineer processes, and so on. Doing any or all of those activities won't mean anything unless you bring value to your enterprise. In reality, you probably should not be performing *any* activity unless it is consistent with your company's business strategy and thereby delivering value. As the information chief, it is also your responsibility to ensure that the resources of the information office are efficiently deployed. The efficient use of the assets under your management also brings value to the company.

As CIO, you must focus on the benefits of technology to your business partners. It is your job to educate the business leaders on the value that complex technologies will have on their business processes. Build cases that explain the benefits from a perspective familiar to your senior management team. The successful CIO, as a custodian of the corporation's IT strategy, is required to bridge any gaps in understanding the benefits of technology between the IT organization and the other business units. There are a number of tactics you can employ. One tactic will be to develop a governance structure that determines *which* IT projects will be selected and managed. You will also need to look at strategic sourcing, which is the process for determining *how* the IT projects will be resourced to accomplish their mission. In other words, will it be sourced internally, with existing systems professionals, or will it be outsourced to a third party with a specific expertise that may be lacking in your organization. Let's look at some of the ways your information office can bring value to your company.

Information Technology Governance

Let's start with the mechanism for determining how technology will be used in the enterprise. That structure is known as IT governance.

What is information technology governance?

It is a mechanism to manage IT initiatives at a broad level. IT governance is a vital part of corporate governance in today's information economy. The primary purpose of governance is to generate alignment of the IT strategy with the business strategy. IT governance usually consists of a set of organizational structures, processes, roles, and responsibilities. It is a set of basic ground rules that guide information technology to ensure that it is consistent with the objectives of the business. There are many driving forces for developing a governance process. You may ask yourself, "Why do I need IT governance?"

Let's examine some reasons.

> <u>**Scarcity of IT resources**</u>. There is generally a shortage of two types of IT resources in an enterprise: dollars and people. If the availability of IT systems professionals is not the problem, then they may not have the specific skills needed to accomplish the necessary tasks. Like any asset of the

corporation, the allocation and use of skills, knowledge, and money will need to be maximized.

Changing cost and availability of technology. As more and more technology choices become available, as technology continues to improve over time, and as more and more technology companies are created, the price of technology will continue to decrease. The governance process will need to address how the company should strategically exploit the changing cost of technology. The governance model should allow for the appropriate allocation of that technology across the business units.

Collaboration across business units. I mentioned previously how the increase in demand for IT services is occurring as the dependence on technology increases. Often, the business products and the information systems are one and the same (e.g., in the financial services industry). We have also discussed how the IT resources are becoming scarce. This will naturally cause conflicts between business units as each area attempts to successfully fulfill its strategic objectives. There are also some IT products and services that will be specific to a business unit while other products and services are common to all. This will require a prioritization of both business and IT processes, which by default requires collaboration across the company as a whole. The result should be the effective and efficient allocation of scarce IT resources to the activities most beneficial to the business.

An increased requirement for consistency. One of the many complaints that both internal and external users of IT services has is a lack of consistency in development practices, in service delivery, in expenditures, and in skill levels. This lack of consistency can lead to a lack of confidence in the IT organization. A governance process can help improve consistency through the agreement of the information office and the business units about how projects can be managed and how the IT processes and business processes will interact.

Adherence to corporate and/or regulatory policy. The Sarbanes-Oxley Act has placed a great deal of pressure on the IT department, as well as other areas of the company. In addition, many companies have strict regulatory guidelines to which adherence is critical (e.g., the airline industry). A governance process can ensure the entire portfolio of IT initiatives across the enterprise follows these policies. This could prevent the company from incurring huge penalties for violating these policies and regulations.

This is by no means an exhaustive list, but it should give you an idea why having an IT governance process could assist you in achieving your goals. Now let's look at an example of a governance model.

One of the more popular governance models is known as the federation model. This is frequently used in very large organizations. These organizations usually have both a centralized IT function as well as an IT function within each business unit. In addition, the enterprise is structured into relatively autonomous business units. The model looks something like this:

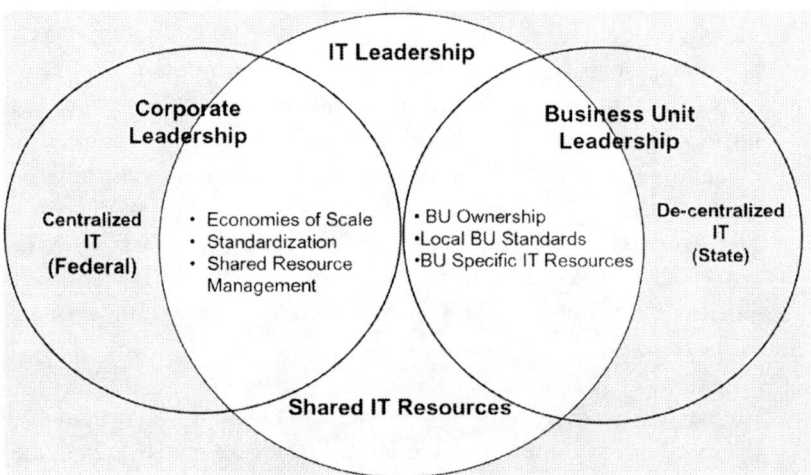

Figure 8. Federated IT governance model.

I chose this model because it is both common and complicated. This model has a governance board that is made up of representatives from the corporate leadership team, which includes the central IT leadership function. In addition, the governance board contains representatives from both the business unit (BU)-level IT function and the BU-level business areas. This model requires a great deal of participation, and it can get large and cumbersome. Many organizations counter this by *not* including BU-level business units, per se. Instead, they have representation (or advocates, generally executive vice president-level people) from the corporate leadership team.

The advantage of this model is that, after decisions are made, they are understood by everyone. This minimizes future conflicts on the use of technology resources. This approach requires defining the decision boundaries for the federal and state domains, creating a conflict resolution process, and maintaining an excellent communication path between organizations.

There are many different types of governance models, organizational structures, and processes. You should adopt one that is consistent with your IT organization and the company's strategic direction. Suffice it to say that some type of governance model should be established within your organization. This will ensure that the IT resources are optimized by the company, and the IT activities are consistent with the company's strategic direction.

Information Technology Strategic Sourcing

At this point, it should be clear that how an organization defines, plans, and manages the deployment of its IT resources and services is extremely important to ensure the continuous achievement of its business strategy and objectives. Strategic sourcing is emerging as an effective process to meet this goal. The company should use a combination of internal and external resources to dynamically align the business requirements to IT sourcing options. The primary purpose of this approach is to provide agility in fulfilling the objectives defined by the governance board. Okay, what does all of this really mean?

It means that you will not always have the skills necessary to complete your strategic objectives. It could also mean that the required skills and talent are only needed on a temporary basis. Your strategic sourcing alternative is to assemble the internal talent, determine what is needed, and then acquire the talent shortage from an external source, perhaps a consulting company that specializes in the area where you have a talent shortage, an outsourcing company (if your needs are more long-term), a vendor partner that you are currently using, or maybe even another department within your company. This technique allows you to quickly build a team of qualified participants without concerning yourself with whether the necessary talent is currently in your organization. You may even strategically outsource some work to free up the talent that already exists in your organization.

When we talk about products and services, strategic sourcing allows you to purchase the best IT products and services for the best value. Your purchases will not necessarily be from only those vendors with whom you currently do business. Instead, *any* vendor can provide you the quality, quantity, and compatibility, as long as it is at the best price. When you use this purchasing approach, you must first analyze what you are buying. Then you must analyze the current market conditions. Finally, you must determine who can supply those specific products and/or the services that you require. Use all of this information to select the best values available in the IT marketplace. Strategic sourcing in reality is *competitive sourcing*.

In summary, the purpose of strategic sourcing is to achieve the maximum benefit from the IT resources, as well as the resource suppliers. This will bring a tremendous amount of value to your company without compromising quality or service.

The Final Word on Value

We live in a time when budgets are tight, competition is strong, resources are scarce, and success is sometimes measured in basis points (i.e., the smallest measure used to quote yields on bonds and notes. One basis point is 0.01 percent of yield). As a result, there is an intense focus on the bottom line and the need for quantifiable evidence of IT value. The standard IT measures that you will use will not always communicate your value to senior management. This will be a challenge during budget time when it will be necessary to justify why that significant chunk of the company's financial resources (i.e., your budget) should continue to exist at its current size. More importantly, senior management will question whether your budget should be reduced. Processes such as IT governance and IT strategic sourcing can provide the roadmap that will outline to your budget stakeholders the value they will receive and how that value will be achieved. You should also establish business metrics to communicate your value effectively with your business partners. Some ideas can be found in the section entitled, "If You Can't Measure It, You Can't Manage It."

Remember, IT is more than likely *not* your company's primary business. If you are not providing a value to your company that you can demonstrate and that they can see and understand, then the reason for your existence is questionable.

CIO—"Career Is Over"?

Is this really true? Is this the end of the line? Does CIO really mean, "Career is over"?

Of course not.

It is true that the life span of a CIO seems to be relatively short, in that people don't seem to stay in that job very long. The average tenure is about eighteen to thirty-six months. It is also true that many people have failed in that job (obviously they didn't read this book). Of course, the definition of failure is somewhat subjective. If you continue to follow the careers of people who are no longer CIOs, they have a tendency to move on to bigger jobs with more responsibility. Successful former CIOs outnumber the CIOs who have never been heard from again.

Let's look at the numbers. As of this writing, there are over 140 million people in the workforce in the United States. Within that number, there are approximately 6 million people who work in the information technology profession. There are approximately 260,000 people in computer management positions.[2] Globally, those numbers are even more impressive. It is estimated that there are only about 20,000 people in the United States who hold the title of CIO or fill the position (whether they have the title). That means that you are a member of a group that makes up about 0.14 percent of the workforce. That is a very elite group. That also means that there is an extremely small percentage of people on this planet who can do what you do. Why, you ask. Just look at chapter 3. Look at the amount and diversity of skills required to do this job. Simply put you—and the people like you who fill the position of CIO—are very unique!

I like to think of CIO as meaning, "change implementation officer" because there are a tremendous amount of changes that you now have the opportunity to implement—changes in processes, strategy, technology, and changes in the bottom line when all the other changes have been implemented. You now have the unique opportunity to impact your company.

I asked a number of current CIOs to give me their definition of the acronym CIO. Here is what they said:

> *"Chief Intelligence Officer"*—*Jerry Crenshaw, CIO*

> *"Chief Idea Official"*—*Terry Miller, Professor of eCommerce Kaplan University*

---

2 Bureau of Labor Statistics for occupation code 11-3021—Computer and Information System Mangers

"Chief Influence Officer"—*Steve Printz, CIO*

"Chief Infrastructure Officer"—*Ron Jones, CIO*

"Chief Ingenuity Officer"—*Rob Adams, CIO*

"Chief Investigation Officer"—*Wayne Kaplan, CIO*

"Chief Independence Officer"—*John J. Lignowski, CIO*

The CIO is required to learn a great deal about the company and how it operates. In addition, the CIO must help develop and work within the company's strategic objectives. There are not many professions within the company that get the exposure to the business operations as the CIO does. These things make the CIO an extremely valuable individual to the senior management. This has allowed many CIOs to grow into positions outside the information technology area. For example, one of the CIOs that I used to report to in United Airlines was promoted to chief operating officer (COO) of the airline. At the time, United was the second largest airline on the planet.

So, if anyone ever approaches you and tells you that CIO means "Career is over," just smile and walk away. You will know that they don't have a clue about what it takes to do your job. More importantly, you will know that there is a high probability that they *can't* do your job! Just look at the numbers.

Things Are Changing (And Will Continue to Change) Faster Than You

On April 19, 1965, an electronics engineer by the name of Dr. Gordon E. Moore wrote an article for the *Electronics* magazine. At that time, Dr. Moore was considered a new breed of electronics engineer. Dr. Moore was the director of the Research and Development Laboratories of the Fairchild Semiconductor Division of the Fairchild Camera and Instrument Corporation. In reality, he was one of the founders of Fairchild Semiconductor.

Dr. Moore opened the article, entitled "Cramming More Components onto Integrated Circuits," by writing:

> The future of integrated electronics is the future of electronics itself. The advantages of integration will bring about a proliferation of electronics, pushing this science into many new areas.

> Integrated circuits will lead to such wonders as home computers—or at least terminals connected to a central computer—automatic controls for automobiles, and personal portable communications equipment. The electronic wristwatch needs only a display to be feasible today.

He goes on to say:

> Computers will be more powerful, and will be organized in completely different ways. For example, memories built of integrated electronics may be distributed throughout the machine instead of being concentrated in a central unit.

Dr. Moore was a true visionary. When he wrote this article, we did not have personal computers, cell phones, computers in cars, or any of those other things that we consider commonplace today. In 1965, he also predicted that by 1975, there would be a whopping 65,000 components on a single silicon chip. The most famous observation made in 1965 by Dr. Moore is known today as Moore's Law.

Dr. Moore observed that the number of transistors per square inch on integrated circuits had doubled every year since the integrated circuit was invented. Moore predicted that this trend would continue for the foreseeable future. The actual trend slowed down a bit in subsequent years. However, data density has doubled approximately every eighteen months. It is this growth trend that has been affectionately defined as Moore's Law. It remains popular even today. Dr. Moore himself has personally validated both this definition and trend. The opinion among IT experts is that this trend will continue for at least another couple of decades.

By the way, Fairchild Semiconductor—which Dr. Moore founded—is now called Intel.

The processing speed of high-performance computers has consistently increased at an annual rate of 60 percent, doubling every eighteen months, or a hundred times per decade. In 1971, Intel succeeded in putting 2,000 transistors on its first computer chip, the 4004. Today, the chips contain over 1,000,000 transistors. Many computer and materials scientists believe that the number of transistors per chip will continue to increase over the next forty to fifty years, despite the growing cost of fabrication facilities and likely changes in building-block materials, architectures, and lithography techniques.

The demands of cyberspace (i.e., the Internet), entertainment, and other commercial businesses drive the quest for greater computing power. If past trends continue, the operating speeds of high-performance computers in 2035 are expected to be in excess of 1 petaflop (i.e., 10^{15} floating point operations per second) and memory size will be 10 terabytes. It is estimated that the human brain has a processing power of 1 petaflop, so computers in 2035 may well become personal assistants that provide a high degree of intelligent support. In other words, your personal computer will probably be your best friend!

There is a belief among some scientists that the physical limitations of the current technology will challenge Moore's Law in the coming decades. The reason is that current chip makers use a process known as photolithography (i.e., patterning and etching chips using light sources). Many believe that this process is limited by the wavelength of light. Therefore, the process may not be sustainable over the long haul. Unfortunately, as CIO, you will *not* be able to breathe a sigh of relief. The reason is that the use of extreme ultraviolet (EUV) lithography, which is the leading replacement candidate, will be available for production by the end of this decade. This will help manufacturers move the product from the .18 micron level today to levels below 65 nanometers (nm). In addition, nanotechnology is promising to be the long-term answer to the photolithography problem and will allow Moore's Law to continue well into the future.

The Forbes/Wolfe Nanotech Report entitled *Nano 101: An Insiders Guide to the World of Nanotechnology* defines nanotechnology as "the precision placement, measurement, manipulation, and modeling of sub—100 nanometer—scale matter, or matter that consists of about 4 to 400 atoms." A nanometer is one billionth of a meter or 1/75,000th the width of a human hair. As mind-boggling as it may be to talk about working at the molecular and atomic levels, it is a reality that will expand the limits of current computer technology. You will continue to be faced with technology growth challenges. At this point, the magic is in thinking small!

In looking at the growth of computer technology, it is also important to look at the status and developments in software languages that allow computers to perform applications. The evolution in software has been from assembly language to more-compact, higher-ordered languages, which has resulted in an improved productivity. This growth is measured in average cost per function point of about 5 percent per year. Although I am not a great proponent of function points, their use is fairly widely accepted. The size of software application tasks (i.e., complexity) has continued to grow at a rate similar to the performance gains of computers (i.e., at 60 percent per year). My personal experience in high-transaction environments like the airline business has clearly demonstrated the same growth in complexity.

Most software applications development efforts take, on average, about a year to eighteen months to complete. The complexity in hardware and the subsequent application software complexity will increase at the aforementioned rates. That means that software development runs a risk of being the Achilles' heel of the adoption and/or implementation of information technology growth. In other words, by the time an application development effort is complete, the underlying technology on which it was built would have experienced a significant change. So the newly completed application could be implemented on old technology. In addition, the error rate in code development also increases with the size and complexity of programs. This compounds the productivity problem.

What does all of this mean to you? As CIO the technologist, you need to understand that the growth of technology and the subsequent increase in demand for complex software applications will probably outstrip your ability to satisfy that demand. That is, if we assume that normal development techniques are employed. Fortunately, the technology demand in any one company is generally not at the same rate as the growth in technology as a whole. At this point, are you beginning to wonder if you can be successful? Not to worry, all is not lost.

As CIO, your job is to understand this rate of growth and the rate of growth of all of the technologies under your auspices. You must stay abreast of these changes and anticipate the impact on your company's strategies and plans. The true challenge will be to anticipate where the technology is going and to gear your development efforts to *meet* the technology at implementation time. In addition, you should only plan to employ technology consistent with your corporate direction and strategy. This will narrow your scope and ensure the continued value of your organization to the company.

To Outsource or Not to Outsource—Not a Real Question

You are the new CIO of your organization. You are excited. After about twenty-six nanoseconds, you realize the honeymoon is over. How do you know that? In the first meeting with your senior executives, they have explained to you—with great clarity—how the IT function is dysfunctional and too expensive. They also make it excruciatingly clear that you need to significantly cut costs, increase service, and improve performance. By the way, while you are at it, the morale of the IT department could use a little improvement too! Sound familiar?

Your first thought is, "I need to talk to an outsourcing company, fast!"

Of course, your conversation with that executive could have also been about how the outsourcing decision that had been made three years ago doesn't seem to be working. Performance has not improved, it is taking just as much time (or longer) to develop application systems, and the cost of this outsourcing contract seems to be a lot more than was originally thought. "We thought that the 'outsourcing thing' was supposed to save us a lot of money. We just don't see it. In any case, you need to fix it!"

Here your first thought, again, is "I need to talk to an outsourcing company, fast!" (Although I suspect the conversation would be a little different.)

So, based on the two scenarios, is outsourcing a good thing or a bad thing? The most decisive answer is…it depends!

What Is Outsourcing?

In a nutshell, outsourcing is the process of moving business functions to a third party in the hopes of improving operations and service, cutting costs, focusing on the enterprise's core competencies, or, often, all of the above. Just about any business function can be outsourced. As far as the IT business function is concerned, companies have outsourced applications development, help desk functions, data center operations, desktop computer maintenance and service, network management…Well, I think you get the idea.

Why outsource? The primary reason to outsource is that the value proposition of outsourcing is very compelling in a resource-constrained economy. As revenues decrease and expenses and competition increase, business leaders seek to leverage proven outsourcing techniques to accomplish even more with less. Often, companies have had to lay off skilled systems professionals because of capital constraints. This may leave the company short of skills needed to make progress with IT development projects or technology opportunities. Acquiring the skills from a third party that specializes in IT services could be a cost effective solution to this problem.

Outsourcing can also be compelling in a resource-rich economy as well. Surrendering an organization's IT function, in whole or in part, to an outside service provider can be very rewarding. It can improve your company's income statement by reducing the cost of performing that function. It can also strengthen the corporate balance sheet by converting unneeded (or sometimes unwanted) IT assets to cash. If you are in a company where IT is not your primary business, then more than likely it is also not a core competency. What better way to free up capital for investment in your core business than to outsource nonessential functions? In this case IT could be considered a nonessential function.

Outsourcing also comes in different flavors. Outsourcing can be onshore or offshore. Onshore is relatively easy to understand. It is outsourcing to a company in the same domestic region as you. For example, if you live in England, an onshore outsourcing provider could be located in London.

In offshore outsourcing, many companies seek to cut costs and increase efficiencies by entering into outsourcing arrangements with foreign companies. These are generally referred to as "offshore" companies. Many companies in India, Asia, South America, and the Philippines have established outsourcing services in their economies. These companies provide a variety of IT services. The most prevalent services are call center operations, applications development, and maintenance. Offshore outsourcing may present many advantages to companies, such as lower cost of labor, a density of technology professionals, and laws that promote foreign direct investment through the provision of outsourcing services.

Outsourcing to foreign companies can often raise issues that outsourcing to a domestic company would not. For example, there could be language difficulties, challenges with securing the company assets in the event of a disaster, and legal and regulatory compliance issues both within the foreign country and domestically.

As CIO the strategist, your decision to outsource should include whether to outsource to an onshore provider or an offshore provider.

Some Challenges with Outsourcing

A common mistake with outsourcing the IT business function is expecting to ignore your responsibility for the function and the IT vendor after the contract is signed. In other words, feeling like "It is the vendor's problem now." Wrong.

The fact that you have now outsourced the function does not mean that you can sit back with you feet on you desk and dream up all of those great things you did not have time to think about before. You didn't really eliminate work. What you did was change the nature of your job.

First, you have a mind-set change that has to take place within your organization. The reality is…it is your job to change it. Here is an example of what I mean. Last week, your business partner in accounting called your programmer, John (her favorite programmer), whenever she wanted a new column put on the monthly ledger report. Of course, since John has known her for years, he would always accommodate her. John is now an employee of the service provider as a part of the outsourcing deal. So when your business partner in accounting calls John (as she always has done), now you begin to hear the faint sound of a cash register opening. You hear that sound because you know that each of those calls costs the company some ridiculous hourly rate for this highly skilled systems resource. That's right, the same John who always has one side of his shirt hanging out of his pants and his glasses on crooked. Yes, the person you always thought had low social needs. He is now a highly skilled system professional who costs you a lot of money whenever you call him. Your job will be to make sure that the corporation understands this new environment. You must establish a set of controls (uh-oh, the C word) and strict procedures for working with the vendor. I assure you, this will not be easy. Habits have been developed. Changing the way people think and operate is always difficult.

Remember that increased service and improved performance you were going to get from this outsourcing deal? Remember all of the money the service provider said you were going save? How do you know if you are achieving service levels or saving on your IT costs? Do things just feel better, so you're okay? Are you going to ask the vendor? Are you going to ask you business partners in the other business units? How will you know?

Whether you have outsourced all of your IT functions or a part, you now have to create a service management function to manage the relationship with the new service provider. The functions, which are now outsourced, must be properly managed with effective contract and service-level reviews to ensure that expectations and business objectives of the deal are realized. You have to monitor the billing, the service levels, and the costs, and manage the new business process. You need to set up a governance process so that both you and the vendor understand your roles and responsibilities and how you will operate in the new environment. Then that governance process needs to be managed.

So, you see, some organizational and procedural challenges still remain, even though you have outsourced the functions. You have established a new relationship that must be managed and have changed the way your company does the business of IT. It is your job to manage that relationship and establish the new way in which your company provides its IT products and services.

What Is Insourcing?

Insourcing is the opposite of outsourcing. You may already have an outsourcing contract with a service provider. For whatever reasons, it may not be working out exactly as you expected. It could be that things have just changed enough within the industry or within your own enterprise that it is time to consider bringing some of those outsourced services back inside. That is the concept of insourcing.

Keep in mind that IT outsourcing providers have steadily built a profitable industry through adopting highly efficient service delivery tools, processes, and procedures and by leveraging their assets. There is no real magic associated with doing that. By implementing the appropriate tools and techniques, you can transform your IT service delivery environment to be as efficient as the vendor. You can achieve the same level of savings an outsourcer would promise to provide. Sometimes all you really need to do is to analyze the processes and procedures that you provide, improve upon them, and begin to duplicate the type of efficiencies that the outsourcer is delivering. This sounds like a job for your change agent personality!

One Last Word on the Outsourcing/Insourcing Thing

As an executive, the outsourcing or insourcing decisions you make will have a profound impact on your company…and most likely, your career.

Outsourcing was originally used simply to save money. Now outsourcing is expected to contribute significantly to an organization's efforts toward higher quality, increased efficiency, greater value, and consistent customer fulfillment and satisfaction. For example, companies that outsource applications development usually look for a provider that is rated CMM (i.e., Capability Maturity Model) level five. This indicates that the company has a set of system development processes that meet a high standard. It also indicates that those processes are repeatable. There is generally an expectation of increased efficiency from the executive team of that company.

Outsourcing can also result in a loss of control and in-house expertise. This happens because most outsourcing contracts have provisions that allow the outsourcing provider to purchase the IT asset (which includes the people asset) from the company. This could leave the company with little or no in-house IT skills.

The decision to outsource is a long-term decision in a short-term world. It is a decision that can seem absolutely essential to an organization committed to focusing on its own core competencies or reducing its costs. At the same time, it could present frighteningly difficult problems. You should perform a thorough analysis of your internal IT business processes, your IT costs, and the outsourcing providers before making your decision.

In any case, one thing that you should always keep in mind is that even if the final decision is not to outsource, the result of the analysis process will identify potential business improvement opportunities. After all, that is what you are really after anyway!

Okay, so now your analysis is complete. But you already have an outsourcing contract. IT outsourcing and service agreements, like the one you have, are generally long-term contracts spanning many years. As a result, the outsourcing decision, once made, should be reviewed constantly. There will be constant changes in your business environment, the industry, technology, the availability of resources, and so forth. You may have simply improved your internal IT processes significantly. At some point, as the CIO, you may decide that a way to increase value to your enterprise is to insource some or all of the IT functions. Interestingly enough, the reasons to insource may be very similar to your initial reasons for outsourcing. In that, the service performance from your vendor may not materialize as expected; there may be more hidden costs than expected so the anticipated savings are not being realized; or, customer satisfaction may not improve.

So whether to outsource your IT functions is not a real question. As the enterprise CIO, you should be agnostic when it comes to outsourcing. The question is what decision makes the most sense in supporting the business objective, whether that objective is to save money, improve efficiency, improve customer satisfaction, or focus on core competencies. Maybe the thought process should be called *right-sourcing*. In actuality, as the CIO, you need to develop an IT sourcing strategy to truly add value to the business enterprise. Your strategy must give you the ability to quickly manage a dynamic mix of internal and external IT resources based on a set of ever-changing industry, business, and technical conditions. Consider the IT products and services that may be strategic to the company and keep them within the enterprise. You just may need to insource those functions back into the enterprise if they have already been outsourced. In addition, your strategy should analyze those IT products and services that can be considered commodities and/or are not within the core competencies of your IT organization. Those functions could be targets for outsourcing. In other words, you want to focus your intellectual capital on those functions that you do best.

Whichever decision you make, some of your internal business partners may not think the solution is the correct one. If you have made the decision based on the overall business objectives of the enterprise, you should be able to provide a compelling argument to the majority of the stakeholders.

Maintaining Skill Levels—"Weed and Feed"

"Great vision without great people is irrelevant"

—Jim Collins

One of the most challenging aspects of a CIO's job is maintaining the appropriate skill levels of your IT professionals in the ever-changing technology environment. You need to keep in mind, now that you are the CIO (even if it just happened yesterday), your executive team expects that you are fully versed on all of the different technologies, development techniques and methodologies, and software. Of course, you and I both know that is impossible—unless you have a big red S on your chest that you have cleverly hidden under your shirt…can change your clothes quickly in very small, discreet places…and have a habit of jumping over very tall buildings when no one is looking. If so, this will be a piece of cake. If none of that is true, then one of your most challenging jobs will be to keep your team current on all of the technologies that are appropriate for your organization.

In his best-selling book *Good To Great,* author Jim Collins talks about making sure you have the right people on the bus. He says that if the right people are on the bus, it will be much less of a problem if we have to change direction (Collins, 2001). In other words, you need to ensure that you have the right people on your team to be successful in executing your strategic plans…even if those plans have to change. I strongly support that idea. I also believe that many times we have the right people on our teams but they have not been properly developed to handle the tasks that we have assigned them. This sometimes manifests itself in insecure behavior. You have an extremely competent person on your team who can handle just about any situation or decision that is handed to them. Yet instead of displaying that competent behavior, they bring every problem and situation to you to make the decision. They seem concerned about whether they will be fired if they make an independent decision. They demonstrate that behavior even though you (and the person) know that no one has ever been fired in your company for making a less-than-perfect decision—at least not in your organization. In any case, the net effect is a slowdown of progress while the situation waits for your intervention.

There are a number of reasons why this could occur. In the past, you may have demonstrated micromanagement behaviors that make people feel that you have to make all the decisions. The company could have a risk-averse culture. This behavior could have developed over time. Regardless of the reason, your immediate impression may be that you have the wrong person on the bus. This may not be true. You may just need a behavior change of a person who clearly *does* belong on the bus.

I have a technique that I use to overcome that insecure behavior. I ask the person, "If you were me, what decision would you make?" Then (assuming the decision is not totally off-base and is close to the decision I would have made), I say to them that their decision matches the one that I would have made and that they should proceed with its implementation. After two or three encounters like this, the person usually starts to feel like they are wasting their time and mine, and will begin making decisions on their own. Eventually, my job is to council, guide, and give advice on those decisions that required some slight adjustments.

Will this work for everyone on your team? Absolutely not. But for those who are truly the right people for the team, this has proven to be a good development tool. It also saves you the amount it costs to replace one of your most valuable team members. That cost is generally about 150 to 200 percent of their annual salary.

Unfortunately, you will also learn that not everyone belongs on the team. This means that some will not be able to bring any real value to fulfilling your strategic direction. This may mean that you will have to rotate people off of your team to make room for people who have the desired knowledge and skills. Make room for the people who will be able to help you move forward on your strategic plans. This technique for removing and replacing people is commonly known as "Weed and Feed."

Now that you have the right set of people, what can you do to ensure their success? Their success can be ensured by a clear set of well-established, repeatable processes.

The Striped Team Story

I thought that the following short story would be a good lead into the next section. It is entitled, "The Striped Team." After you read it, you need to ask yourself whether this depicts your people's feelings about the way things work in your organization. If so, then your change agent personality needs to go to work.

Enjoy!

THE STRIPED TEAM

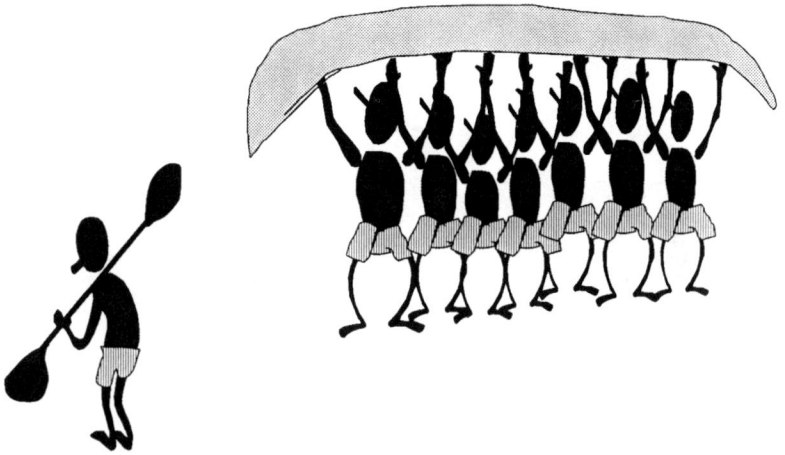

Once upon a time there was a Stripped rowing team.

This Stripped team agreed to hold an annual rowing race with a Square team. Each team would contain 8 men.

Both teams worked hard to get in the best shape, and, on the day of the first race, both teams were ready to win.

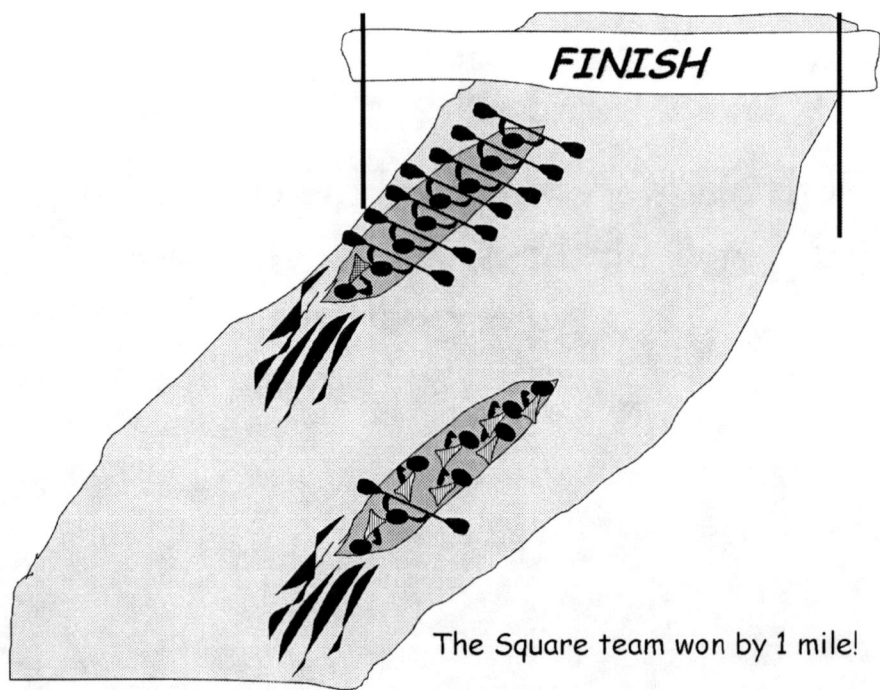

The Square team won by 1 mile!

The Stripped team was crushed in their defeat, but they were determined to win the race next year. So they established a panel of auditors to observe the situation and ascertain if there were any differences between the teams.

After several weeks of detailed intelligence gathering, the auditors could find only one difference: the square team had seven rowers and one captain…

...and the striped team had seven captains
and one rower!

Un-perplexed by the raw data, upper management showed unexpected wisdom: they hired a consulting company to analyze the data and suggest a solution that would enable the Stripped team to win next year.

After several months, the consultants concluded that the ratio of captains to rowers
was the problem of the striped team.
Based on this analysis, a solution was pro-
posed: the structure of the striped team
needed to change!

Upper management wasted no time in restructuring the striped team into four captains, led by two managers, reporting to one senior director with a dotted line to the rower. In a blaze of inspiration, they also suggested they might be inclined to improve the rower's working environment by a non-monetary reward and recognition scheme if there was improved performance by the rower.

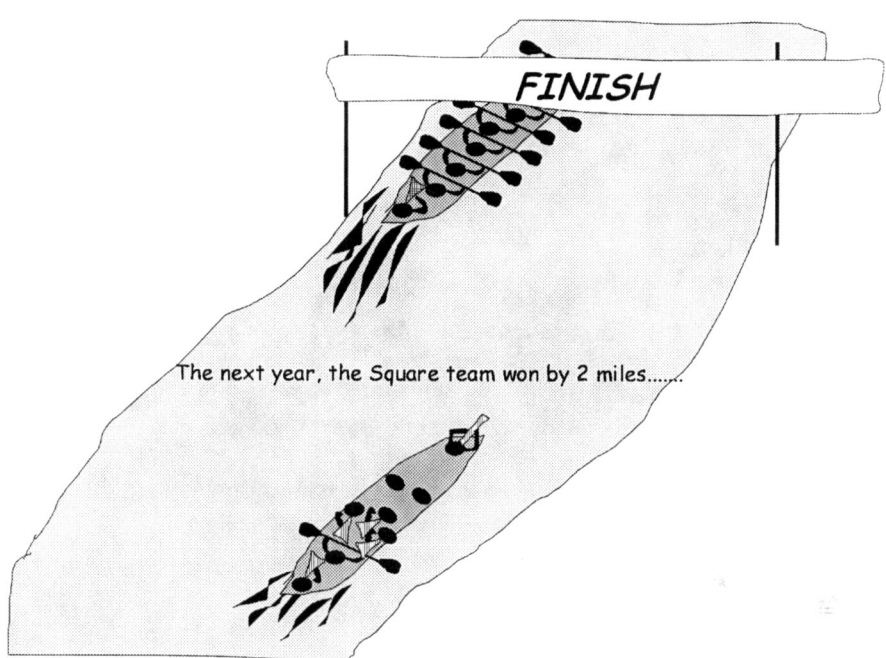

The next year, the Square team won by 2 miles........

The Stripped team's upper management immediately fired the
rower based on his unsatisfactory performance.

A bonus was paid to the Captains, Directors, and Managers for the strong leadership and motivation they showed during the preparation phase and as an incentive for them to find a better rower for the next race.

The consulting company prepared a new analysis of the restructuring activity, which showed that the strategy was good, the motivation was great, the restructuring was executed correctly, but the tool used (which was not included in the original data) was substandard and had to be improved.

The striped team management had a new boat designed; and to demonstrate fiscal and HR dexterity for stockholders they also contracted a placement agency to advertise in other countries for a new (temporary, nondirect employee) rower.

The End

(of The Striped Team)

Lots of Processes...Very Few Processes...What?

"It takes less time to do a thing right than explain why you did it wrong."
—Henry Wadsworth Longfellow, Poet (1807–1882)

A process is an organized collection of behaviors performed according to a specific, well-defined set of targets and outcomes to meet a defined business purpose. CIOs constantly ask themselves whether processes help them to get things done or hinder their overall operations. Effective processes provide a framework for achieving your goals and objectives. They also establish a consistent, repeatable set of services that bring value to the company. On the other hand, a poorly defined and poorly executed set of processes will slow progress, confuse the business, and do little to assist the company in achieving its strategic direction.

The literature that exists about the number of processes, methodologies and procedures available for IT is enough to make all of your CIO personalities *go crazy*. The processes you decide to use should have only one key objective: to support the strategic direction of the company. Any processes that you implement to effectively manage the IT environment should tie directly to the processes used by the business. Robert S. Kaplan and David Norton in their book *The Balanced Scorecard* define a framework that companies can use to establish their business strategies. If your company uses this approach, then you should create an IT scorecard that supports and integrates with the business scorecard. If your company does not use Kaplan and Norton's scorecard approach, then create a set of IT processes that integrates your processes with the processes that your company uses. The key is to be able to demonstrate, in business terms, the contribution and value that IT is making to the company and its overall business objectives.

As you might have guessed, there are different processes for the different aspects of your IT operation. This can be confusing. I have organized the different processes that should concern you into two primary categories: *financial* and *IT internal*. These categories will assist you in managing IT like a business unit rather than just a service center. They should also help you align your IT processes with your company's business processes.

Financial

Financial management is one of the fundamentals of good corporate governance. As CIO, you will have fiduciary responsibilities over a significant amount of the company's finances. You will need to be concerned with the detailed financial management of IT development projects, operational systems, and IT services. In most cases, you will be responsible for managing tens of millions, if not hundreds of millions, of both capital and expense dollars. Your IT budget could represent anywhere from 1 to 5 percent of the corporate revenues and a larger chunk of the corporate expenses. This is enough to keep your financial personality quite busy. If you are not careful, this could dominate a great deal of your time at the expense of all of the other activities that require your attention.

Along with your normal budgetary responsibilities, you will also be responsible for the operation of the company's accounting and financial systems. It will be your job to ensure that these systems are producing the highest quality of output. In other words, the results of these system operations must be accurate, complete, and up-to-date. The increased legislative focus and requirements (e.g., Sarbanes-Oxley) will put pressure on you and the IT department to have an effective IT governance and set of processes that protects your company's financial information. Finally, as CIO you will be constantly expected to demonstrate your value to the enterprise, including rationalizing your investments in new technologies. All of these items dictate sound financial processes within IT.

It will take a tremendous effort to develop meaningful IT financial processes if your company is like most other companies. The challenge will be worth the effort, but this is not the time for you to be creative. You should be prepared to use the same techniques to value the IT investments as the company uses for all other investments. Some of the techniques that you could use are Total Cost of Ownership, Total Economic Impact, Return on Investment, Return on Infrastructure or Assets Employed, People/Cost ratios, just to name a few. You will need processes (that probably already exist in the company) to capture the data, establish the standards, measure the variances, report on the results, and correct any unfavorable variances in a meaningful amount of time. By using your company's existing financial processes, you have a greater chance of tying the IT financials to the business financials, and this will help validate the value of IT to the company. In addition, it eases the communication with the senior management team about the progress you are making in executing your IT strategy. This is primarily because you will be speaking in their language.

IT Internal Processes

As CIO, you will have to concern yourself with two types of internal processes: systems development and operations.

Systems Development

Software (or systems) development processes have been around for over fifty years. The systems development environment is a specific effort to automate the business processes by using hardware, software, people, and procedures. There are two models of software development in which all of the systems development processes are based. The first model is sequential development, in which one activity follows the completion of the one before it. The second model is an evolutionary process, in which an iterative technique is used to develop the system. There are basically two approaches to systems development within those models. First, there is a process-oriented approach. This approach focuses primarily on information flow. It follows the transformation and use of data through both the manual and automated system. The second most common approach is data-oriented systems development. This approach depicts that ideal organization of data, independent of who, where, or how the data are used. The majority of the system development methodologies today are based on one of these two approaches.

Some people believe that you should have a process and/or development methodology—such as Agile, eXtreme Programming (XP), Rational Unified Process, traditional (waterfall) process, etc.—for each type of development work and maintenance work that you are doing (e.g., small projects, large projects, proof-of-concept projects, technology-oriented projects such as distributed vs. mainframe, maintenance projects, etc.). Others believe that you only need one process regardless of what you are trying to accomplish. Of course, others believe that all of the process stuff is just a waste of time because all it does is take more time.

Unfortunately, the cold reality is that only about 10 to 20 percent of IT projects come in on time and within budget, regardless of the process technique that is used. In most cases, systems development projects are not only late and over budget, but are likely to be cancelled. If they are not cancelled, then the final software product rarely meets the expectations of the users for whom they were built. This is not a good track record, no matter how you look at it. Using a consulting firm for your systems development or buying commercial off-the-shelf (COTS) packaged software does not seem to improve the odds of success either. There is a general consensus that the high failure rate is a process problem rather then a technology problem. The IT organizations that use the traditional processes will say that the reason for so many failures is that the requirements are always changing. The people who adhere to the rapid, agile process approach will say that this is nonsense. They say that change is inevitable; therefore, any process that is used should be flexible enough to accept changes. They argue that the real problem is that most processes try to have clear, predictable results in an environment that is unpredictable.

I believe that, regardless of whether you adopt one of the traditional approaches or use an internally developed methodology, the effective use of processes is as essential to the development of systems as the methodology that is used to develop the company's strategic plans. It allows for predictability, consistency, and sometimes agility in the development process. If you do the following, this is especially true:

1   The process is adopted by the organization;
2   Taught throughout the organization; and
3   Consistently followed.

In addition, your organization could be assessed at a higher CMM level (see "Capability Maturity Model" in the Glossary) if these steps are consistently followed. A company that does not use any methodology at all would be assessed at level one, the lowest capability level.

Let's examine some of the systems development processes a little more closely.

Systems Development Life Cycle. The systems development life cycle (SDLC) process consists of multiple phases that help manage a wide range of activities to automate business activities using information technology. The SDLC is not limited to technical activity but begins with customer needs and evolves through processes and user requirements to develop a solution or support process. The process ends with maintenance activities. The final solution should always include a way to use a feedback mechanism for continuous improvement of the newly established business procedures and automated systems. There is also another phase of the systems development life cycle that is usually left out. It is a phase that is consistent with the life cycle of any asset (see "CIO the Asset Manager"), that is, the disposal or sometimes called *sun setting* the system. The life span of software systems is becoming shorter and shorter. The criteria for when the life of a system should end should be established at the time it is built. Over time, that will alleviate the current problem of the huge inventory of legacy systems that exists.

A SDLC generally has about six or seven phases, depending on the methodology used. As you may have guessed, there are numerous methodologies for the development of systems or new businesses processes. Some methodologies are formal approaches that have been around for many years. Others have been developed by consulting firms to sell to their clients. Still others have been developed internally by companies and then distilled over the years so that exactly how each phase of the SDLC is to be performed within that company is clear. I will highlight a couple of the more popular systems development approaches.

Traditional SDLC (Sometimes Called the Waterfall Approach)

This methodology has a defined set of phases, usually six or seven, that follow in sequence. The phases sometimes overlap, which is what gives it the *waterfall* effect. It is called the traditional SDLC because its origin dates back as far as mid-1960. There are many institutions, both in the public and private sectors, which still use this approach to systems development. Most of the methodologies in existence today are based on the traditional SDLC approach to systems development. The following depicts a typical set of traditional SDLC phases:

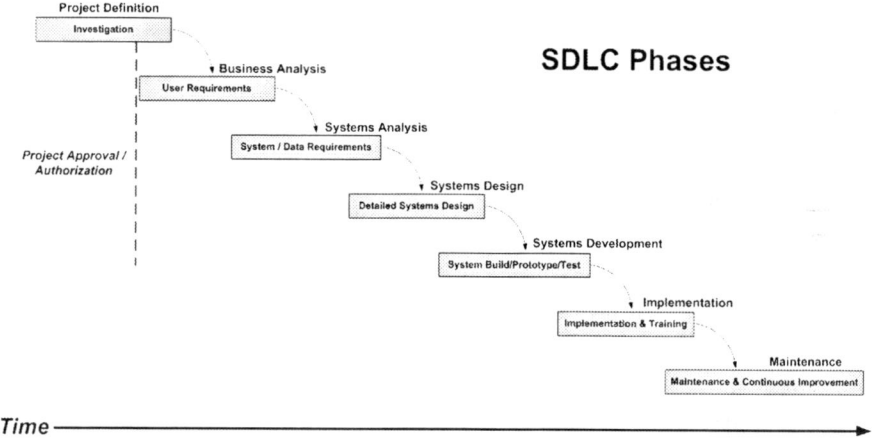

Figure 9. Example of traditional systems development life cycle (SDLC) phases.

Rapid Applications Development

One of the methodological beliefs is that some of the SDLC steps within the various phases can either be removed or shortened, primarily the systems analysis, design, and development phases. Based on the system that you are trying to develop, you may not need to perform all of the SDLC steps. You could perform some of the steps more rapidly, using development tools that would significantly compress the development time. That gave rise to the concept of Rapid Applications Development or RAD. Rapid Applications Development was introduced by James Martin in a publication with the same title (Martin, 1992). RAD is more a concept than an isolated process in itself. It uses the traditional SDLC as its basis for systems development.

RAD is noted for its considerable amount of user involvement, which is characterized by the use of the Joint Applications Development (JAD) technique. A JAD is a series of meetings or workshops held with business users to obtain requirements, clarify design, demonstrate prototypes, and resolve issues. RAD is also noted for its use of various modeling and prototyping techniques. In addition, Computer-Aided Software Engineering (CASE) tools are sometimes used by RAD projects to provide automated assistance to the development phase of the project.

Today, virtually any methodology that shortens the systems development process is considered a RAD methodology.

Structured Systems Development
Structured systems development is also a top-down development approach that is based on the traditional SDLC. The systems analysis, design, and development phases of the traditional SDLC correlate with the structured analysis, structured design, and structured development phases of the structured systems development approach. Although this is a top-down methodology, it evolved from the bottom up. It started with structured programming, and then the structured design techniques were developed, followed by structured analysis. This methodology was made popular by Edward Yourdon in mid-1970 in the numerous publications that he produced on the subject.

Structured systems development was a very popular approach. Like many of the earlier methodologies, it addressed the "hard" development problems with little or no focus on the "soft" (i.e., people) issues. It had its primary emphasis on the maintainability of program code and improved visibility of program design. This methodology is not used much today. Many of its techniques have been absorbed into other methodologies.

Object-Oriented Systems Development
I have a cat named Trash...If I were trying to sell him (at least to a computer scientist), I would not stress that he is gentle to humans and is self-sufficient, living mostly on field mice. Rather, I would argue that he is object-oriented.
—Roger King "My Cat is Object-Oriented"

Object-Oriented systems development is a combination of both process and data-oriented approaches to systems development. This approach views the real world as objects as opposed to the traditional systems development that tends to view it as processes and programs. In addition, the traditional method separates the data from the processes that use it. The object-oriented approach suggests that data and processes cannot be considered in isolation, but instead depend on each other and must exist as a single unit. Like structured development, object-oriented development is used primarily during the analysis, design, and programming stages of systems development.

Object-Oriented development uses a modeling process that progressively develops a representation of a system element (or object) through the phases of analysis, design, and implementation. The model is abstract in the early analysis stages of development. Then, as the model evolves, it becomes more and more detailed. One of the more popular object-oriented modeling techniques is called the Unified Modeling Language (UML). UML allows the modeler to specify, visualize, and construct the business models as well as the components of the software system.

Rational Unified Process (RUP)
The Rational Corporation developed the Unified process. The Unified Software Development Process (generally called Rational Unified Process or RUP) has been considered a potential solution to the problem of software development failures. This approach is unique in that it is use-case driven, architecture-centric, and uses an incremental, iterative methodology. The Unified Process provides guidance to the order in which system development activities are performed. It also directs the tasks of individual developers and the project team as a whole, specifies what artifacts should be developed, and offers criteria for monitoring and measuring a project's products and activities.

RUP is characterized by two dimensions: the horizontal axis, which represents time and shows the life cycle development phases of the process, and the vertical axis, to represent core process workflows, which are logically group activities. Each development phase has one or more iterations that are designed to produce completely functional portion of the system. The following is an example of the Unified Process phases:

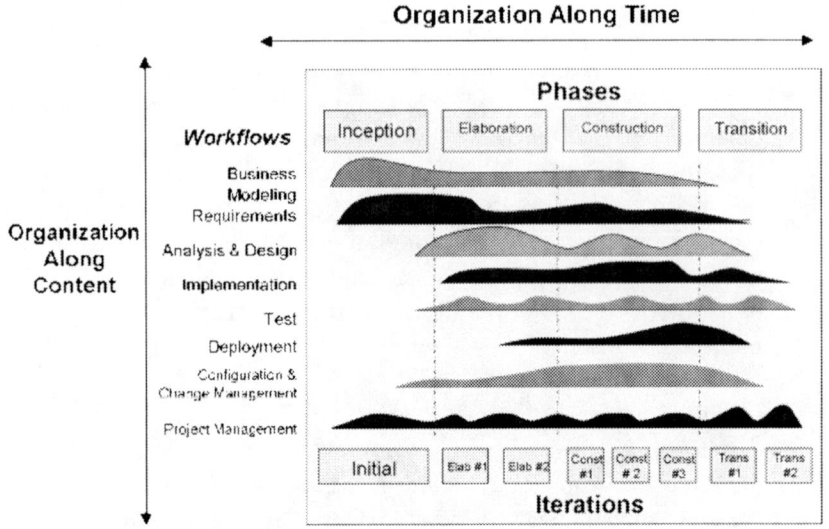

Figure 10. Example of Unified Process phases.

Agile Systems Development

Agile software development is not really a specific development method like the other methodologies, but instead a family of methodologies. It is a conceptual framework for undertaking software development projects.

There are many processes that have claimed to be agile methodologies. In the late 1990s those methodologies began to receive an increasing amount of attention. A number of organizations have also developed what they considered their own *lighter* approach to building software, but they all have certain characteristics in common. Regardless of the method or approach used, all emphasize a close working relationship between the development team and business users; face-to-face communications versus written documentation; frequent delivery of new, usable business value; and self-organizing teams. The following is a list of approaches that are considered agile methods:

- SCRUM
- eXtreme Programming (XP)
- Dynamic Systems Development Methodology (DSDM)
- Adaptive Software Development
- Feature Driven Development
- Crystal Clear Method
- Rapid Applications Development (James Martin)
- Pragmatic Programming

In early 2001, a group of industry experts in agile development met to outline the values, principles, and unifying theme of their methodologies. They called themselves the Agile Alliance. The result of the meeting was the manifesto of the Agile Alliance. The following is the Agile manifesto that can be found on the Agile Alliance Web site (see the "Web sites and Magazines" section):

We are uncovering better ways of developing software by doing it and helping others do it. Through this work we have come to value:

- **Individuals and Interactions** over processes and tools
- **Working Software** over comprehensive documentation
- **Customer Collaboration** over contract negotiation
- **Responding to Change** over following a plan

That is, while there is value in the items on the right, we value the items on the left more.

The next product of the Agile Alliance after the manifesto was created was the principles of agility. The principles allow software teams to develop systems quickly and respond to change. The following are the Agile principles which also can be found on the Agile Alliance Web site:

1 Our highest priority is to satisfy the customer through early and continuous delivery of valuable software.

2   Welcome changing requirements, even late in development. Agile processes harness change for the customer's competitive advantage.

3   Deliver working software frequently, from a couple of weeks to a couple of months, with a preference to the shorter timescale.

4   Business people and developers must work together daily throughout the project.

5   Build projects around motivated individuals. Give them the environment and support they need, and trust them to get the job done.

6   The most efficient and effective method of conveying information to and within a development team is face-to-face conversation.

7   Working software is the primary measure of progress.

8   Agile processes promote sustainable development. The sponsors, developers, and users should be able to maintain a constant pace indefinitely.

9   Continuous attention to technical excellence and good design enhances agility.

10   Simplicity—the art of maximizing the amount of work not done—is essential.

11   The best architectures, requirements, and designs emerge from self-organizing teams.

12   At regular intervals, the team reflects on how to become more effective, then tunes and adjusts its behavior accordingly.

Unlike the traditional SDLC methodology, the agile methods frequently produce completely developed and tested features. These features are produced every couple of weeks or months and are a subset of the entire system. As a result of this approach, these methods have been successful when used on small development efforts containing ten or fewer collocated development team members. I have not found many successes on larger projects.

Component-Based Development (CBD)

Component-Based Development (CBD) is an approach where software applications are assembled from components from a variety of prepackaged generic elements. It is essentially constructing a system from prefabricated parts. This development model is sometimes referred to as Component-Based Software Engineering (CBSE). In either case, the objective is to control the cost of software development while increasing the quality of the end product. The components of CBD may be written in several different programming languages and may run on several different platforms. Like a number of other methods, CBD attempts to improve the design, construction (or development), and implementation phases of the SDLC. Each component in CBD is designed to be deployed independently. A component has an external specification, which is independent of its internal operations.

One of the key advantages of Component-Based Development is that the components needed for the systems development effort already exist. Unfortunately, this means that a separate development process is needed to identify and create the components that will be used in future systems development efforts. Sometimes this creates a challenge to determine what components will be needed and then to develop, test, and store the completed components. Once created, a process and standards also need to exist for the development teams to access and use the completed components.

Another key advantage of CBD is that the systems developers may not require a high level of skills, since the complex components already exist. The only requirement is to ensure that the assembled parts can work properly together in the new system.

Software Configuration Management. The created software is a vital asset to the company. Processes must be in place that can locate the original source code that created the software system, identify who has changed that software, provide a mechanism for maintaining all of the changes to the software, and allow any previous version of the software to fall back if an event occurs that warrants such action. The process that handles these activities is called Software Configuration Management.

Companies have experienced problems with software that is operational in their production systems. They are dismayed to find that it is almost impossible to correct the problem. Changes have been made to the source code, and it no longer reflects what is running on the production systems. The problem is further exacerbated when they find that there are no records of the changes that were made. It is the CIO's responsibility to ensure that good configuration management processes are in place to prevent such situations from happening in your company.

Business Process Reengineering (BPR). There are other processes that exist that are not necessarily a part of the SDLC but can help to improve the systems development endeavor. Many are used to outline, define, and improve business processes; define and analyze workflow; and/or restructure organizations. One of the more mature approaches is Business Process Reengineering or BPR.

Businesses constantly face a changing environment. Companies merge and acquire other companies at a staggering rate. The numbers of companies outsourcing their business processes to reduce costs has steadily increased over the past decade. Many large companies need to reduce their size and eliminate their bureaucracy to compete with the smaller, boutique enterprises that are encroaching on their market share. All of these forces—and more—are causing companies to reinvent or reengineer themselves to survive. BPR helps a company determine what it should look like once it has executed their strategy to accomplish one of the aforementioned changes.

There are a number of different BPR approaches. Each of them basically has four phases. The first phase looks at the current state of the organization or business unit. The objective is to determine its "as is" view. The next step is to determine the "to be" or future view of the organization. In other words, assuming no restrictions, "How *should* the organization look?" The next phase is to develop a process to move from the current state of the organization to the ideal future state. The last phase in the process is to determine the practicality of phase three. This means that this step determines the cost to complete the transition, the obstacles that may hinder the transition process (remember, the future state is an *ideal* view), the establishment of possible alternatives, and a definition of the most probable future state of the organization.

IT Operations

I always think of the data center (which includes the network) as a utility. I like to make the analogy that it is like the power company. People don't usually make a habit of calling the power company after buying a new lamp to determine if enough power exists at the plant to operate the lamp. They assume that the power exists and that there will be enough to operate the lamp. There is an expectation that when the lamp is plugged in and turned on, that the light will come on. Likewise, people in your company will operate their businesses with the expectation that the data center will be there, and that all of the required facilities will be available and operating properly. In other words, the data center is transparent to their operations like the power plant is transparent to our daily activities. In both cases, that transparency is eliminated when the expected services are not available. It is imperative that stringent processes are put in place to ensure that the utility remains transparent, regardless of the business strategies that are employed.

The processes associated with IT operations are numerous. Failure to implement any one of these processes could be extremely detrimental to the business, as well as to the successful fulfillment of the business strategies. Let's take a look at each of them.

Network Management. If we use the analogy that an organization can be considered a body, then the network is the veins, and the information the blood that flows through those veins. Today networks come in a variety of sizes, scopes, and architectures. They range from a simple dual-node local network to a complicated, encrypted network, connecting tens of thousands of nodes all over the planet. Regardless of the size, scope, design, or type of network, the network is vital to the operations of the business. Any damage to the network is damage to a vital organ of the business. It is imperative that an effective network management process be in place to ensure the health of the organization.

There are many components involved in network architectures. The great thing about technology today is that it is extremely reliable. But networks still contain components, and components will—and do—fail. Unfortunately, there is no way to predict exactly when failure will occur. The key to a good network management process is knowing when a failure has, in fact, occurred; knowing which component is the culprit; knowing the impact to the business (i.e., the severity of the damage to the body); and, of course, being able to quickly recover from the failure and return to a healthy state.

Your network management process needs to maximize the availability and reliability of the network and its components. You need to ensure that it is available when the business needs it, that sufficient capacity exists to handle the needs of the business, that it is secure from malicious attacks or inadvertent errors, that it is performing at a level that is responsive to the business, and that it is reliable (i.e., that it does not have frequent outages). Your business partners should not have to constantly think about the network, just like you don't constantly think about your veins.

Data Center Operations Management. If you agree with the idea that the network is the veins that keeps the information of the business flowing, then the data center would be the heart that pumps the information through the veins.

I have managed a number of data centers in my career. It never ceases to amaze me how little people think about, or understand, the millions of operations and hundreds of detailed processes that occur there every day. I guess, like the hearts in our bodies, if there is no real problem, we just don't think about the millions of detailed operations that it must perform each day. Don't get me wrong. The fact that people don't think about the data center on a regular basis is a good thing (remember my earlier analogy about the power plant). That generally means that it is operating efficiently enough for people to get their work done and effectively enough to support the business objectives.

There is a set of standards that was originally established by the Central Computer and Telecommunications Agency (CCTA) in the United Kingdom. That standard is called the Information Technology Infrastructure Library (ITIL). The ITIL (pronounced *it tell*) is a set of interrelated best practices. Its purpose is to lower the cost and improve the quality of IT services delivered to the users of the data center services. The ITIL standard is currently managed the by the Office of Government Commerce (OGC) in the UK. Many companies use the ITIL standard set of processes to manage their data center operations.

Let's take a look at some of the processes that must be in place for us to achieve the goal of allowing people to forget that the data center exists.

Performance Management
This process is focused on creating methodical and predictable ways to improve operational results of the data center. Managing data center performance involves both monitoring and tuning activities. Monitoring entails keeping track of the behavior of the systems using a variety of tools and procedures to categorize, identify, and report on that behavior. The ultimate goal of monitoring is to be proactive about any data center performance issues that may arise. Tuning the data center involves the

processes required to change the data center resources (e.g. operating system, data base management system, etc.) to improve overall performance.

Availability Management

The cost associated with business downtime continues to rise. In addition, the growth in Internet and intranet computing has increased demand for system availability. Availability management entails systematically undertaking preventative and corrective maintenance of IT services, within a justifiable cost. This process describes, manages, directs, and proactively maintains the availability of data center services at a reasonable cost and in accordance with agreed-upon quality levels. The key to availability management is to plan for availability by concentrating on the failures that could impact it. This means that you must isolate the overall service functionality from the failure of any individual component. This is usually accomplished through component redundancy. Availability management ensures that the operational requirements of the business are met.

Incident Management

This process manages the entire course of problem solving for all incidents that occur. An incident is any deviation from the agreed upon system or service levels. The purpose of incident management is to provide business continuity by restoring the operational system or service as soon as possible after an episode has occurred. The process generally involves detection, isolation, classification, diagnosis, resolution and recovery of the incident. An overriding objective of incident management is not to allow the incident to occur in the first place.

Problem Management

A *problem* is defined in ITIL as a condition that has been defined and identified from one large incident or many incidents exhibiting common symptoms for which the cause is unknown. The purpose of the problem management process is to investigate and resolve the root causes of faults and disruptions that affect the data center operations. Once the problem is defined and the root cause is determined, then a solution is put in place to prevent the problem from reoccurring.

Change Management

This is a structured method for handling changes to the resources in the data center to ensure that the modifications to the production environment are coordinated and implemented without disruptions. The objective of this process is to introduce change into the data center environment rapidly and with minimal disruption to service. This process needs to be an ordered, well-managed process. It must reject changes that will potentially disrupt operations. It also needs to have the flexibility to address emergency changes that are vital to the business operations. An effective change management process uses the technique of staging. That is, the updated software and/or hardware exists first in a test environment, then a preproduction environment (sometimes called the staged environment), and then, finally, into production. This allows the change to be well observed before it is placed into the protected production environment. In addition, an effective process identifies all affected systems and processes before the change is implemented to mitigate or eliminate potential adverse effects of the change.

Configuration Management

The purpose of this process is to ensure that all appropriate and necessary steps have been taken to guarantee that modifications and upgrades to the data center systems (usually hardware) do not negatively affect system performance, reliability, or availability. This is accomplished through a process that has an implementation plan, a basic test plan, and a back-out strategy if the modification or upgrade is not successful. The process also includes notifying and coordinating with the affected business users.

Capacity Management

This process tracks the usage of the data center resources and anticipates the necessary upgrades required to support the business's expanded usage. As the business grows, the demand for the resources in the data center will grow. This process will predict that growth and ensure that that the necessary improvements are put in place before they are needed. Of course, the trick is to do this without prematurely or unnecessarily incurring additional costs to the business.

Release Management

This process facilitates the introduction of software and hardware releases and ensures that they are planned, tested, and implemented with little or no disruption to the business. It works closely with the change and configuration management processes.

Storage Management

Storage systems can be a small set of tape drives, a disk subsystem, or a complex, geographically dispersed, networked system. Storage management is concerned with both onsite and offsite data storage. Its primary purpose is data restoration and historical archiving. It also makes certain the physical security of backups and archives.

Data Center Chargeback. Of course, there is one time, other than an outage, when the data center is always in clear view…at budget time. There is always a great deal of pressure to cut the operational costs in the data center. The CIO will experience more intense pressure in an organization that has a process to charge back the cost of the data center operations to the business units. This means that at the end of the year, the cost to IT of operating the data center is essentially zero. The business units absorb the total cost of operating the data center. Unfortunately, this process is generally very complicated, due to the number of data center components that are included in the calculations.

The primary challenge with data center chargeback is ensuring that you can effectively capture all of the cost components. The next difficult task is to develop an equitable allocation of those costs. In other words, a small business unit should not have to pay the same amount as an organization ten times its size. Therefore, you will need to have precise usage statistics.

I worked in one company where we charged back our services to the business units. As a result, the business mandated a reduction target of 10 percent of our operating costs each year. There were many years where this was not a problem, given the constant reduction in technology cost,; increases in performance, and significant increases in reliability (which reduced the number of times we had to replace components). As the intelligence of the technology also increased, we were able to reduce the number of people that were required to operate the data centers. We even provided the business with one data center that was a lights-out operation that had no people in it at all. But there were also years where achieving the cost-reduction goal was a little tougher. In any case, we generally achieved the cost objectives while continuing to process over 15,000 transactions a second.

Positive technology trends have existed for decades and continue to exist today. Therefore, the pressure to reduce cost and increase the efficiency of the data center will continue while maintaining high levels of availability and reliability. A tall order? Yes. But, it *is* achievable.

Hardware Deployment Management. Companies today have hundreds and sometimes thousands of desktop and laptop computers. These assets will be managed through the asset life cycle just like all other assets. The life cycle of this hardware tends to be a lot shorter than the mainframe computers and many other assets. This is due to the rapid change in the technology that is used by these systems. For a CIO, the constant redeployment of desktop hardware is just short of controlled chaos, since they were not all purchased at the same time. One technique for managing this environment is to have a process that predetermines when the hardware will be replaced. This is usually called a refresh strategy. Here's how it works. The hardware is analyzed to determine the approximate cycle at which major changes in its technology takes place. For example, there are generally significant changes in desktop computers approximately every three years. A plan is created when the hardware is purchased to replace (or refresh) it at the end of the three-year technology cycle. This technique also helps with budgeting, since the point in time when the capital expense will be generated is predetermined.

The CIO also needs to have a process for keeping track of this equipment because of its ubiquitous nature. Some companies place barcodes on their equipment, while others use a check-in, check-out process for infrequent laptop users. Regardless of the process you use, this environment would quickly get out of hand if you do not put a process in place early.

Business Continuity Management. This process is established as a strategy to keep the business operational during a major event or disaster. This plan is separate from the Disaster Recovery Plan, but it works in concert with that process. The Disaster Recovery Management process is intended to restore a location to operation after a disaster or major event has occurred. The Business Continuity Process (sometimes called Business Crisis Management) keeps the business operating while the recovery is underway. The key point is that Business Continuity Management is a business issue that supports the ability of the business to exist during a crisis or highly disruptive event. These business functions are usually performed at an alternate location. It is the responsibility of the CIO to ensure that all of the key systems and infrastructure services needed by those business functions are operational at the temporary site. The business continuity strategy also consists of plans to reestablish the business functions once the crisis has ended.

Disaster Recovery Management. As mentioned in the previous section, the Disaster Recovery Management process is intended to restore a location back to operational efficiency after a disaster or major event has occurred. It consists of planning the activities that will allow a company to return to an acceptable state of operation after a sudden, unplanned, catastrophic event that causes damage and/or physical loss. Disaster Recovery Management recognizes the potential severe damage to the infrastructure and physical plant from these unforeseen circumstances that can seriously impair mission critical business operations. All possible disastrous events cannot be known; however, it is imperative that the CIO put contingency plans in place to ensure the restoration of the data and information asset as soon as possible when those sudden events do occur. This will ensure the continuation of critical business services and key organizational work processes. The CIO must make the survival of the organization certain when events occur that are outside the control of the company.

Information Security Management. Information security management is the safeguarding of one of the corporation's most valuable assets. Today, data and information are the foundation upon which many corporations, both big and small, are built. As previously mentioned (see "CIO the Security Chief or CSO"), it is an extremely important function of the CIO. This function has many different aspects that must be managed by the CIO.

Vulnerability Management

The primary aspect of vulnerability management is to detect information usage behavior as vulnerability. The management processes must be able to compare the suspected behavior violations to security policies to determine if there is vulnerability in the overall security management process. If it is determined that vulnerability exists, then the process must be able to put a remedy in place to eliminate it.

Identity/Access Management

Computer hacking is on the rise. Studies conducted by the Federal Bureau of Investigation (FBI) and other organizations suggest that the financial losses from unauthorized penetration of computer systems are also increasing. The companies whose systems have been violated generally do not report the violations for fear of adverse publicity. It is also frequently determined that the violator is someone who resides inside the company. The CIO needs to have an identity management process that recognizes the following:

- Who is trying to access the systems?
- What do you know about them?
- Are they internal or external?

- What data, if any, are they allowed to access?
- Does your process contain audit trails of what they have accessed?
- Who, if anyone, approved their access rights?

Access Management provides the appropriate people in the organization with access to the information necessary to do their jobs. It is a process that needs to know when attempts are made to access information. The process must be able to identify who is attempting to or who has accessed the information and exactly what they are accessing. The process must ensure that the actions of the person accessing the information are recorded. This process also needs to ensure that the accessed data is appropriately protected.

Privacy Management
The increasing use of computers and sophisticated information technology, while essential to the efficient operations of business, has greatly magnified the harm to individual privacy that can occur from the collection, maintenance, use, or dissemination of personal information. The data contained in the corporation's databases is increasingly becoming the personal information of individuals. This is primarily due to the significant rise in e-commerce and online buying patterns. It is essential that the CIO have processes in place to ensure that the personal information of people using the organization's information systems is well protected. This also includes information about employees that is kept in corporate information systems.

Security Incident Management
An unexpected or unplanned event may be a breach in security. This could happen through a combination of intrusion attempts, system failures, power failures, or inadvertent errors. The process to manage this is known as Security Incident or Event Management. The process identifies, monitors, records, and reports breaches in data or system security. It is the responsibility of the CIO to immediately act on such breaches to mitigate damage and alleviate the problem. As a member of the senior management team, it is also the CIO's responsibility to notify and make certain that the senior management team is kept up-to-date on the status of the incidents. For example, if the breach was intentional intrusion, the CIO may need to work with the chief legal council, since there is a possibility of prosecuting the offender.

Threat Management

Viruses, worms, spyware, and corporate espionage are all potential threats to the security of your enterprise systems. They can disrupt operations, can cause countless hours of productivity loss, and can even cause a loss of business. The CIO must ensure that the IT environment is protected from these threats. As CIO, you need to have a process that can detect any anomaly or suspicious behavior, inoculate against the identified threat, determine if the threat reveals vulnerability, and determine if the Threat Management process has the ability to respond to the threat.

Compliance Management. Compliance Management means that the CIO is responsible for making sure that the IT environment is in compliance with all internal corporate policies and regulations, external governmental regulations, and privacy regulations. You have already seen how privacy is a security management issue. It is also a compliancy issue. The Privacy Act of 1974 was enacted to protect individuals from harm that can result from the wrongful use of information that is collected and stored in information systems. The company can incur significant penalties and possible loss of business if the CIO does not have a bulletproof process in place to protect the personal information stored in the corporation's computer systems. This is just one of many examples of situations that require the CIO to be involved with compliance management.

In Summary

There are many processes that will be of concern to you. Some will be more important to your company than others. Some are necessary for you to effectively manage the IT operation. Other processes will protect the company from intrusion, disaster, or inadvertent harmful errors. But any processes that are used are only effective if you have established a well-defined set of metrics, on which the processes are based and measured. The processes can be thought of as the scorecard, and the measurement is the score.

If You Can't Measure It, You Can't Manage It!

The title of this section is an age old adage that is still true today. Of course, the first question is usually, "What do you measure?" The answer is simple: *you measure everything!*

You will quickly learn which measurements are important to you and your company and which measurements are not. Although you will be measuring everything, you will only focus on a few key measures. This is no different than what the business community does everyday. There are hundreds of business measures in every company; however, if you talk to any CEO, there are usually between five and ten key measures that they look at on a regular basis to determine the health of the organization.

There are two reasons for having measurements in IT. First, you need to measure things that are internal to the operations of your IT organization. This gives you a clear understanding of how your business is operating, and you can effectively manage the business of IT. Second, you need to measure the IT external operation. That is the impact that your IT organization is having on the rest of the company. This measurement is used by your company to effectively manage its business…and of course, you. Both types of measurement are usually referred to as IT metrics.

Internal Metrics

I consistently refer to the "business of IT" in this book. I strongly believe that IT should be managed like any other business function. Although this may seem intuitively obvious, it is my observation that, in many instances, this has not been the case.

Most business functions, such as sales, marketing, and finance, have a key set of metrics they use to measure their operation. At a glance, they can determine the health of their organization and its processes. For example, in sales one of the metrics may be the number of cold calls that were made in a week versus the number of sales that were closed for the same period. For the production area, it may be the number of widgets produced verses the amount of waste created when the widgets were produced. Finance will be concerned with the amount of revenue generated versus the amount of expenses to create that revenue with an acceptable difference known as profit. There may be many different measurements that each of these areas collect from their various processes, but each unit boils those measurements down into a key set of metrics that each unit monitors on a regular basis.

That is also true of the IT department. There are a tremendous number of measurements collected in IT. These measures are generally based on systems performance over some period of time. There have been numerous books written on this subject, and I will not attempt to duplicate the established literature in this section. However, here are a few of those measurements, just to give you an idea of what they are:

- Average number of MIPS (million of instructions per second) in the data center
- Transaction throughput (i.e., number of transactions per second processed by each host computer)
- E-mail message traffic
- Number of network packets handled
- Number of CPU cycles
- Number of network sessions
- Response time
    - Workstation response time
    - Internal host response time
- Average number of concurrently processing jobs
- Mean Time to Failure of the host machines
- Mean Time to Repair once a failure has occurred
- CPU utilization
- Service Level Agreements (SLA)
- System performance
- System availability
- Application operational performance
- Network performance
- IT Return on Investment (ROI)
- IT efficiency
- Customer satisfaction
- Call centers
- Customer response times
- Problem resolution time
- Incident management
- Web site traffic

I think you get the idea. This is by no means an exhaustive list. I have managed a number of large data centers in my career. I can tell you that this list doesn't even scratch the surface of what is normally measured in a data center.

You also have software development measurements. Some measurements determine productivity, some measure quality, while others measure progress. In their book *Software Metrics: Establishing a company-wide program,* authors Robert B. Grady and Deborah L. Caswell suggest that you develop a software metrics program strategy. They admonish that:

> A software metrics program must not have a strategy unto itself. Collecting software metrics must not be an isolated goal. Software metrics can successfully be only a part of an overall strategy for software development process improvement (Grady and Caswell, 1987).

Grady and Caswell go on to list the following ten steps to developing a successful software development strategy (Grady and Caswell, 1987):

1 Define company/project objectives for the program.
2 Assign responsibility.
3 Do research.
4 Define initial metrics to collect.
5 Sell [internally] the initial collection of these metrics.
6 Get tools for automatic data collection and analysis.
7 Establish a training class in software metrics.
8 Publicize success stories and encourage exchange of ideas.
9 Create a metrics database.
10 Establish the mechanism for changing the standard in an orderly way.

Your overall objective in developing a software metrics strategy should be to ensure predictability in your systems development process. One of the most consistent concerns I have heard over the years about the systems development process from senior executives is that it is so unpredictable. They say that if they were to build a building they feel that they could almost predict to the dollar how much it will cost, predict to the day when the construction will be completed, and predict, with a fair amount of certainty, the quality of the end product. They complain that cost, completion, and quality in the systems development process are a *mystery*. Your software metrics program should endeavor to remove as much of the mystery as possible. This will mean that you should measure the following things:

- Project development performance
- Number of defects during development
- Number of lines of code developed (not used as much anymore)
- Amount of system rework during development
- Development time based on system size

You will need to analyze all of those measures from both the data center and the software development area and create a set of key indicators that will help you quickly determine the health of your organization. Just like the CFO will ensure that expenses stay at a certain percentage of revenues to ensure that the planned profits are realized, you will need to establish metrics that will ensure your operation runs smoothly. You will need a set of indicators for the data center operations and the software development areas (and any other areas that may be under your auspices). Those key indicators will let you know when things are *about to* go awry, *before* the problem has occurred. This will give you the opportunity to make the necessary adjustments and corrections to keep things on track.

It is important for you to understand the purpose of these key indicators. Are you trying to measure productivity? Are you trying to measure quality? Are you trying to develop a set of predictors to ensure future success in systems development? Or is it all of the above? You must know what you are measuring and why. If you are measuring only for measurement's sake, it will be a tough sell to your IT team. Once you develop these indicators, you need to engage your salesperson personality to convince your team of the reasons for measurements and the intended use of the final results. Otherwise, the quality of the data collection may be suspect. This is especially true if your IT team believes that the reason for the measurement is to penalize them and/or their work.

External Metrics

Each of your personalities will have an array of activities that will need to be measured. That means that you will be inundated with numbers and measures. You must let your strategic personality take charge. Understand the activities that are happening in your company and are important to the corporate strategy. Then look at the measures associated with those activities and develop a set of key indicators that will help you to determine the health of those activities. The metrics should warn you of any impending danger. This will give you time to make the necessary adjustments and corrections. Each year these key indicators could change, based on the strategic direction of the company, even though the underlying measurements may remain the same.

Let's look at an example. Perhaps your strategic personality is aware that the company is planning a major expansion through mergers and acquisitions. Your IT strategic plans say that you will exploit economies of scale by absorbing the processing of the acquired or merged company into your data center to eliminate multiple data centers. This will also eliminate a major expenditure of the company. Your key indicators may consist of capacity, utilization, and utilization growth rate of your current computers; floor space utilization in the data center; network capacity, utilization, and growth rate; and utilization and growth rate of the data center peripherals. This is just a few of the handful of key indicators that you could use. You will know when you need to make a capital expenditure for hardware, software, and/or network upgrade by keeping your eye on these indicators and taking action when they begin to slip out of alignment. This will help your company absorb the merged or acquired enterprises more smoothly. At least the IT organization will not be a hindrance to the process.

One Last Word on Measurement

I have learned that one mistake that many CIOs make is that they have a set of indicators that they developed when they first took over as the head of IT. Then they use those same indicators year after year, even though they may no longer be appropriate for the current direction in which you and/or the company are going. Those indicators essentially become out of sync with the rest of the company. The CIOs find themselves reporting on measures that no one else believes are important. Yes, those measures may or may not be perfectly okay for you to measure the health of your own organization; however, they may have become meaningless to everyone else in the company. Therefore, you should be cognizant of the metrics that you need to manage the business of IT *and* the metrics you need to communicate with the rest of the company based on its current direction. All of your metrics should be reviewed annually to ensure that they are still appropriate for what you are trying to accomplish with your IT organization and/or what you need to support the rest of the company.

The Status Quo Is Not Okay

"Everything is in a state of flux, including the status quo."

—Unknown

What is the status quo?

The economy goes through expansions and contractions. Companies merge and/or acquire other companies. Companies will divest subsidiaries that are not within their core competencies anymore, are not performing well, or are no longer a part of the strategic direction. Some companies will outsource major portions of their business while other companies will expand into new markets. There will be layoffs during slow times and hiring sprees during significant growth periods. There will be new product development by the company while old cash cow products will begin to show less appeal in the marketplace. Some companies will embark on major capital projects while at the same time disasters—some natural and some not—will eliminate key business locations. New regulatory pressures will cause companies to change many of their fundamental operating procedures. New global markets will open up, while companies that were business icons will slowly disappear. The national demographics will change the face of the workplace, while new workplace regulations will change how employees are treated. The availability of personnel will expand tremendously as we move into a global society. There will still be major shortages of key skill groups, as technology changes how things are done. The global consumption of food, energy, and natural resources will continue at an alarming rate. At the same time, space exploration will examine the possibilities of living and working on other celestial bodies.

Can you identify which of the aforementioned situations does not require participation from the CIO and the information technology organization? You can't, can you? I didn't think so. Neither can I. The CIO must avoid going into his or her job with the idea of maintaining the status quo. Do not accept any job where you are asked to maintain the status quo. In today's world, I am not sure I know how you would even identify what constitutes the status quo.

In their book *Creative Destruction: Why Companies That Are Built To Last Underperform the Market and How to Successfully Transform Them*, Richard Foster and Sarah Kaplan tell us that Standard and Poor's Index that was first created in

1920 contained ninety companies. The original companies stayed on that list an average of sixty-five years. By 1998, the average amount of time a company stayed on the list was ten years. The authors suggest that if history is to be our guide, only about a third of today's companies will survive in any economically significant way (Foster and Kaplan, 2001). The point is that companies must constantly recreate themselves if they are going to survive. The CIO and the information technology organization will play a major part in the reformation and renaissance of the company. You will introduce new technologies, new processes and procedures, new business techniques, and, of course, new ideas.

Unfortunately, the one area of the company that has a tendency to maintain the status quo is IT. Many CIOs tend to want to leave things alone (i.e., do nothing) and wait for some miraculous technological breakthrough that will make life easier for them. That mentality will not work in the rapidly changing business environment. You must have the right people, the right technology, the right processes, and the right organizational structure to support the constant flux that will occur in your company. For example, your organization must be structured to support the company. The status quo for many IT organizations is to structure it based on technical domains. You will see organizations with departments such as database, networks, servers, software engineering, and so forth. You would probably agree that IT is a service organization. If that is true, then is organizing by technical domains really servicing the company or is it a structure that will only serve IT? Look at the company's strategic direction, current organizational structure, and IT service requirements, and then organize to truly support the business.

Remember, not only is the status quo not okay, from a business perspective, it will be difficult to determine what really is the status quo.

Organizational Issues

I covered seventeen different personalities in chapter 3 that a CIO must assume at any given point in time. Yet this inventory of personalities is not an exhaustive list. One additional personality to add to the seventeen is CIO the Referee. Unfortunately, this persona is used primarily within the IT department.

Your IT department is generally made up of a number of different areas. The two most dominant areas will be applications development and the infrastructure organizations. It has been my experience, after working for a number of Fortune 500 companies, that these two areas generally have some level of animosity between them. Sometimes it is extremely blatant, and sometimes it is very subtle. Regardless of the intensity, it generally does, exist.

List the top three issues that you deal with most in your job.

1   *"Staff issues between departments"*
2   *"Limited staff and resources"*
3   *"Migration to a new platform"*

Ron Jones, CIO
EastPoint Technologies, LLC

I remember being placed in charge of a global infrastructure organization that had a large number of people who consistently produced superior system and network performance. As a matter of fact, their performance surpassed all industry standards. Regardless of that performance level, the applications development department still referred to infrastructure people as "knuckle-dragging tape hangers." I wanted to put an immediate stop to the use of that reference. Much to my surprise, the reference was so ingrained in the organization that I even heard senior managers make the same comment. This was quite disturbing to me. I was forced to recognize that this situation bordered on being cultural. The only way I was able to mitigate (not eliminate) the negative reference to the infrastructure organization was to use my marketing persona. The organization established a campaign to educate people internally about our performance as it related to the rest of the industry. Before we knew it, everyone, both internally and externally, was talking about our superior performance and continual successes.

You *do not* want to have to use the referee persona. You need to understand how your various departments work together. You must also understand any long-standing ill feelings that may exist. Correct them as soon as you learn about them. These situations have a way of seriously impacting the performance of your IT department as a whole. In addition, situations like this are generally known throughout the company. The credibility of your organization could be tarnished. This will have an impact on your ability to deliver and build strong working relationships with your business partners. It is important for you to know as soon as possible if there are any problems and, if necessary, to put plans in place to turn the situation around. It is difficult for your IT organization to work as team (or be viewed as a team by others) if there is any level of bitterness between the IT departments.

You should also understand how the IT organization is viewed by the other business units. You need to know if the IT organization has any credibility issues inside the company. Is the IT department known for delivering on time and within budget? Or is it considered to be poor at planning and delivery? Is it known for conducting itself in a professional manner? Or is it known for being reckless and aloof? Is it viewed as a strategic business partner? Do your peers think of IT as a necessary evil that is isolated from the rest of the company? It is important that you know how people view your organization, regardless of whether that view is good or bad. You will need to use your marketing personality to establish the image that you want your IT department to portray. You may need to create a campaign to enhance its image if it is already viewed the way you would like it to be viewed. Conversely, you may have to establish a campaign to overcome or replace the current image if it is not what you want.

Finally, it is important to understand and know how your IT organization is viewed by the outside world. How is it viewed by your vendors? Are your vendors constantly bypassing the IT department and going directly to your business partners to sell equipment, software, and services? Are the investment analysts (if you are a public company) aware of the impact of information technology on the company's strategic direction and plans? What about the customers? Do they have any idea of the impact of information technology on the products and services that you produce?

You may not have to (or even want to) change any of these impressions. It is, however, important for you to know and understand them. It will help you understand the personality of your IT organization. It will have an impact on your ability to succeed. You need to ensure that the personality that is projected both internally within the IT department and externally is the one you want to project. The image that your IT organization portrays should be based on a conscious decision on your part, not by accident or default.

Ethics and Ethical Decisions

"Moral choices do not depend on personal preferences and private decision but on right reason and, I would add, divine order."
—Basel Hume 1923–1999

I would be remiss in my responsibility if I didn't have some discussion about business ethics and making ethical business decisions. Maintaining an ethical environment is one of the most important, as well as most difficult, aspects of being a manager and/or executive. There are greater opportunities for a CIO to demonstrate poor ethical behavior or to make less-than-stellar ethical decisions. It is even more important for CIOs to not only ensure that their employees are following an ethical behavior pattern, but to also make certain that the ethical policies of the corporation are followed by everyone in the IT organization. In addition, through the normal process of gathering information during systems analysis, as well as the systems themselves that have been placed in your care, you will be privy to and given access to a great deal of sensitive information. How you handle the responsibility of being entrusted with that information is extremely important. You will need to establish an additional personality, CIO the Ethics Officer.

In his book *Making Ethical Decisions,* Michael Josephson discusses his six pillars of character. Josephson's six pillars include the following (Josephson, 2002):

1 Trustworthiness: honesty, integrity, reliability, and loyalty

2 Respect: civility, courtesy, decency, dignity, tolerance, and acceptance

3 Responsibility: self-restraint, accountability, and pursuit of excellence.

4 Fairness

5 Caring

6 Citizenship

These six pillars are a great foundation for basing ethical decisions and directing employees toward strong ethical behavior.

There has been a lot written in the press recently about various situations in which managers and executives have not demonstrated good ethical decisions. These situations highlight what can happen to a corporation when ethical decisions are not made. The impact on our corporations can be devastating. The impact on our communities can be injurious. The impact on our employees can be harmful. The impact on us, as executives and representatives of our corporations, can be destructive. It is our duty and our responsibility to create and to present the most ethical business environment possible.

Strong ethical behavior is good business. It builds pride in our employees, admiration in our customers, and trust in our business partners and stakeholders. Our ethical behavior also defines our values as a company. It is our duty to establish an ethical set of standards and practices within our company that demonstrate its values. Once established, those ethical standards and procedures must be communicated, internalized, and practiced. Your ethical values will be challenged by peer pressure, project schedules, your personal desire to get ahead, time pressures, competitive pressures, and others' ambitions, just to name a few. When your values are challenged (and they will be), you must *never* compromise.

Insanity Will Want to Prevail

Rita Mae Brown once said that the definition of *insanity* is, "Doing the same thing over and over again, in the same way and expecting different results." Unfortunately, a number of people want to operate in this mode. They do not want to change the way they have been doing things, regardless of whether there is a better way. This may sometimes frustrate you, since you are a change agent. The job of your change agent personality is to look at the way things are currently done and, whenever possible, to improve on it…sometimes using technology.

There are three types of people in the world: those who make things happen, those who watch things happen, and those who wonder what happened! Your change agent persona will want to make things happen while the people who *wonder* what happened will frustrate you. They will sometimes frustrate your efforts as well. Unfortunately, many of these people will be in your IT organization. It has been my observation that most people who stay stuck in their same old ways are simply afraid of change. They are at the beginning of the change cycle (see "CIO the Change Agent"). It is important for you to know where each person is on the change cycle so you know how to deal with them. Let's review the change cycle in a little more detail.

What is the most *difficult* aspect of implementing change in your company?

"Overcoming the 'we have always done it that way' attitude."

Charles Massoglia, CIO
Dawn Food Products, Inc.

There are many different definitions for the phases of the change cycle. The following is a definition based on a great deal of reading as well as observations I have made from my own personal experiences and the behaviors of people going through changes that I have implemented.

Apprehension	In this stage, people generally worry about losing something that they currently enjoy. It could be knowledge of the way things are done, prestige from being an expert about the way things are done, or just comfort with the current process. Regardless of whether people perceive the change to be good or bad, they will feel like they have lost the way things use to be.
Denial	This is the stage where people do not accept the change because they will simply ignore that it has happened or is going to happen. They will miss meetings about the change, fail to respond to e-mails, and ignore phone calls on the subject.
Anger	Once they begin to realize that the change is either going to happen or has happened, they will no longer be nervous about losing something. They will be angry that they no longer have it. These people will appear hostile about the change. They will find every negative aspect of the change that they can dig up. They will also communicate how bad this change is to you and everyone they know.

Depression

In this stage, people realize that the change is going to happen, things will not be the same, and they will experience the loss that they were anxious about losing. These people will generally attend all of the meetings, but they will not participate. They will read the e-mails, but not answer them. They will appear to be unproductive as it relates to the change. They will neither hinder nor help the change process.

Conscious Disagreement

In this stage, people understand the change and what it means; however, they will challenge it because they disagree with some aspect of the change or the entire change scenario. This may also be true of people who are totally for the change. They will challenge how the new process or system will work, how it will be implemented, how it *was* implemented, and so forth. They will endeavor to modify some aspect of the change with a "better" way.

Compliance

For you, this stage represents the light at the end of the tunnel. People can now see the advantages of the change and the possibilities this change has presented to them. They will be positive about the good results that the change will bring. These people will execute the new processes or use the new system as it was designed. You will receive constructive feedback about how the change is progressing. They will spend a great deal of time learning all aspects of the change and developing a strong understanding of how things work.

Acceptance

In this stage, people understand the change and are involved in it. They have identified the benefits of the change and have acknowledged its value. You will hear very little from these people. If you do, it will generally be positive and/or constructive.

Internalization	When people reach this stage, they are no longer talking about or referring to "the change." It is no longer viewed as something different. It is now simply the way things are done. These people have integrated the new process, system, organizational structure, and so forth with all of its successes and failures into their regular routines. A change now will start people back through the change cycle again, since this is now the norm.

These are some possible phases that people go through before and after you implement change. Everyone will go through these changes. The only difference is that some will go through it faster than others. Some charts attempt to predict the amount of time that people spend in the various stages of the change cycle. I will not do that. It has been my experience that it is different for each person. Your concern should be the people who seem to be stuck somewhere in the first three stages. They will frustrate you. This will be especially true if they are in your IT organization. If so, you may need to make a tough decision about them. You will need to examine whether they can be taught to move on through the rest of the cycle or weeded out (see "Maintaining Skill Levels—Weed and Feed").

People who are not in your organization will be a little tougher to manage. In that case, your marketing persona has to take over. You will need to constantly keep people updated on the benefits of the change. They will need to see what is in it for them. It will also be important to keep the leaders of the areas affected by the change updated on a regular basis. You will want them to carry the word to their organizations. This will help ease their people through the change cycle.

In summary, you will need to understand that people will want to demonstrate insanity, simply because they are in the first phases of the change cycle. You will be able to identify which stage of the cycle they are in by the way they respond to the change. For example, if you don't hear anything from them, then they are probably in denial. Prepare a communications strategy that addresses each stage of the change cycle that people will experience. In other words, your communications strategy should try to reach people, regardless of the stage of the cycle in which they currently reside. This should help move them through the cycle quicker and help you to have a smoother implementation. It is imperative, however, that you deal with people as soon as possible. This is especially true if you see that they are stuck in one of the first three stages. If they are in your own IT organization, deal with it immediately. If not, work with your senior business partner to alleviate the situation as soon as possible. You, not insanity, will prevail.

Your People

Chapter

"Anything the human mind can conceive and believe, it can achieve."
—Napoleon Hill

In 1927, the theoretical physicist Werner Karl Heisenberg developed the uncertainty principle. The uncertainty principle states that, at a microscopic level, it is impossible to know both the momentum and position of a particle. To do so you need very sensitive and generally very powerful measurement devices. As a result, those devices must disturb the very system under investigation. We have to look so closely at the thing being measured that we can affect how it behaves. Therefore, we cannot be totally sure of the results of the measurement.

I am convinced that some variation of Heisenberg's principle can be applied to the management of people, albeit not at the quantum level. You can manage people so closely that it affects their natural behavior and their performance. If left alone, they would operate and behave differently, maybe even better. Therefore, what you think you are seeing and measuring is actually affected by you, the observer. So how can you be totally sure about the results of your observations?

This is a paradox of management in general, and the CIO specifically. You will endeavor to attract, hire, and retain some of the best people in the industry. You will assign them to your most critical tasks, believing they will be the best people to make it happen. You will ensure that they have the most advanced tools available to them. You will make certain that they are given the best training possible to guarantee their methods and techniques are honed. Sometimes you will locate them together with other highly skilled professionals, both from within IT and from the business units outside your systems organization. You will expend a lot of the company's capital endeavoring to guarantee the success of those valuable people that you hired.

You will personally manage things because of the importance that you have assigned to them. After all, the organization is counting on you. Unfortunately, you may manage them so closely that you affect the behavior of the people being managed. As a result, you can't truly be certain of the outcome of that critical project. Why? Because your management style is affecting the people assigned to get the project done. This is a variation of the Heisenberg principle at a much higher level than the quantum level.

Scary, isn't it? The question becomes, "What should you do?"

The answer is simple, remember, there is a reason why you hired those particular people.

There Is a Reason Why You Hired Them

"So much of what we call management consists in making it difficult for people to work."
—Peter Drucker

One of the greatest challenges a CIO has is managing stress levels and morale. It is your job to recognize overstressed situations in your organization as well as with particular individuals. It is up to you to ensure that your systems professionals stay motivated (see "CIO the Motivationalist") and that morale stays high. I don't need to go into a great deal of detail on what that does to your ability to execute. Some level of stress is good. Some level of stress is necessary to ensure that the creative juices are flowing and that peak performance is maintained. But, like anything, too much of a good thing can be disastrous. A leader who micromanages the operation can cause an overstressed team. Let's examine this thought for a minute.

Napoleon Hill once said, "Surround yourself with successful people and their success will come back on you."

I truly believe that surrounding yourself with successful people is one of the primary keys to success.

Anybody can read a person's resume, check to see if they have a pulse, and then make them an offer. What about truly understanding their skills? What is their work ethic? What is their work style (or management style)? Does their personality fit with yours? Does their personality fit with your objectives? Are their personal objectives consistent with that of the organization (and you)?

Always endeavor to get the best and the brightest in each discipline that you need. Don't skimp. Don't compromise. Don't settle! Pursue your people needs with the highest level of tenacity that you can muster up. Be prepared to take some time to pursue, select, and hire the right person. It will pay great dividends later on to you, your new hire, and your company.

Once you have surrounded yourself with successful, hardworking, highly skilled IT professionals, there is only one thing left to do…get the heck out of their way! There is a reason why you hired these particular people. These people are good. You know it…and they know it.

Your people will need a leader that is like the conductor of an orchestra. In other words, you need to let them manage themselves. The conductor does not tell the woodwind section how to adjust their reeds. The maestro does not show the percussion section how to tighten their drums. The conductor just assumes they know that part. The conductor ensures that they know how to play together to create beautiful music. The conductor coaches them on when to participate and whether they should be playing loudly or softly.

If you were to examine how managers climbed in the corporation, you will understand why some manage the way they do. Many managers have a tendency to manage people like they used to manage tasks and projects. They would manage people like they were just a component of some larger entity rather than as individuals. Managers should think about what made them successful in the past. Then it will become obvious to them why they manage their people the way they do. Think of the preparation they had before they were given management positions. They were judged to be good management material because they performed well as doers, as technicians, as developers, or even as individual contributors, like trumpet players in an orchestra. That often involved organizing their resources into discrete units of work. After years of managing their work at this level, it is not surprising that they developed people management techniques and styles that are similar. It would be extremely presumptuous of me to think that everyone manages this way. Only you know if you fit into this category.

Unfortunately, this micromanagement technique does not work well on IT people, or any highly skilled people, for that matter. There will generally be one of two outcomes—and sometimes both. Your people will constantly look to you to make every decision and to solve every problem, which, of course, you can't. They will never develop the experience necessary to be good strong IT professionals, and both the morale and stress levels could be negatively impacted. Although difficult to do initially, if this looks like your management style, then you may need to let go of some of your natural tendencies, and let your people do what they are good at doing.

You may remember from chapter 1 that I am a Trekkie. I really like the *Star Trek* series. One particular episode, "The Ultimate Computer," comes to mind when I think about management styles. In this episode, the *Enterprise* is chosen to participate in the secret experimental testing of the M-5, which is a supercomputer designed to replace many of the humans aboard a starship. As a matter of fact (okay, maybe not real fact), the crew of four hundred is replaced with the M-5 and a crew of twenty. The new M-5 is just another one of the brilliant and ingenious creations of Dr. Richard Daystrum, the designer of all of the *Enterprise's* computers. When the M-5 computer is engaged, one of its tasks is to approach the planet Alpha Carinae 2 and to automatically place the ship in orbit. In addition, it is required to recommend the participants for a landing party that will go down to the planet's surface. The M-5 proceeds to approach the planet, place the starship in a precise orbit around the planet, and make the landing party recommendations. Captain Kirk is annoyed to find out that the M-5's recommendations are the same as his—with one exception. He and Dr. McCoy are not included in the M-5's landing party recommendation. Dr. Daystrum asks the M-5 why the captain and the doctor are not included. The M-5 replied that it considered the captain and the doctor "nonessential personnel."

Was the M-5 telling the captain that his participation in the landing party activities was micromanagement? Was it really necessary for the captain to *personally* participate in the landing party activities when he had a crew of twenty professionals who were capable of handling the job? Are you participating in your own landing party when you have a crew that is more than capable of handling the job?

You hired them. They are good. If they are good, then they can manage themselves.

It may be important for you to know why your people should be led by you. You are the maestro. You are the coach. You are the mentor. You acquire the resources they need to succeed. You are their bureaucracy buster. You remove obstacles that could hinder their success.

What is the most *difficult* aspect of implementing change in your company?

"Having to learn the challenges that the IT staff encounters on the day-to-day basis and then finding way to integrate their respective needs with those of the company as a whole."

Charles Murphy Jr., CIO

Now that you've figured out what you should be doing, do them and inspire your team to lead or manage themselves. Your job is not to make all the decisions or even to shoulder all the responsibilities. You should not be ready to answer all the questions—get your people to do that; they are the experts. You must learn how to give ownership of your people's problems to them and then to move out of the way and let the people solve them. You must allow them to take the initiative and seize leadership of their positions and their jobs. You have worked hard to create an organization of self-starters and top-notch people who will see their assignments through to the end. My personal philosophy is that "when I see an IT professional who is able to swim easily, I throw them a bag of rocks!" IT professionals generally like to be significantly challenged. This philosophy has helped me succeed over the years. I have been able to build staffs of very strong professionals. I built a team of professionals that have individually gone on to manage very large, complex organizations.

You still must accept personal responsibility for difficult decisions in your organization. You will also need to directly face the hostility those decisions may unleash. You will need to put certain processes, procedures, and controls in place so that you don't lose control yourself. But in the end, when it comes to the day-to-day leadership of the hundreds—maybe even thousands—of activities that will occur in your organization, you must be willing to put yourself out of a detailed manager job. You must be willing to build so much competence, confidence, and initiative among your employees that *they* can operate your organization, and do it well…almost without you.

I know this sounds tough, maybe even controversial. Just don't forget all of the personalities that you need to take on as the CIO of the enterprise. Then ask yourself, "Can I really be all of those things to all of those people and still manage every detailed task effectively?" I would suspect the answer is probably not.

There is a reason why you hired them. So just let them do their thing.

Stay in the Helicopter

"I learned that a great leader is a man who has the ability to get other people to do what they don't want to do and like it."
—Harry S. Truman 1884–1972, thirty-third president of the United States

I was a technical wizard who worked his way up through the ranks to become a senior vice president of a multibillion dollar corporation. One of the first mistakes I made when I first became a manager was to micromanage my people. Fortunately, early in my career I had some excellent mentors. The first piece of advice they gave me was to stay in *the helicopter*. I figured my career was in trouble because my mentors had lost it! What were they talking about, stay in the helicopter? I am in IT; we don't have any helicopters.

They were really telling me that there is a personality called CIO the Forest Ranger. Your organization will have a tremendous number of things going on. Projects will be underway; equipment will be purchased; strategic planning and execution will happen; you will be weeding and feeding your team. Not everything is going to happen as you would like. In other words, there will be lots of fires everywhere. The only way for you to see the fires (or hopefully the smoke before it becomes a fire) is to get your helicopter off the ground so that the forest (your organization) is in full view. You will only have a clear view of the fire in front of you if you keep your helicopter on the ground. There could be other fires smoldering or raging out of control in your forest that you just wouldn't be able to see.

Your strategic personality requires that you have a broad view of your organization and its participation in the strategic activities of the company. It will be difficult for you to do that if your helicopter is on the ground. At best, you will only be able to focus on one small aspect of the strategy.

We have already discussed the idea of hiring good people, understanding and knowing who they are, and getting out of their way so that they can do their thing. Those people are also your firefighters. That means that their job is difficult on a good day. Both you and your helicopter will simply be in their way if you keep it on the ground. It will also be extremely difficult for you to direct the activities of all of the fires and firefighters in the forest unless your helicopter is in the air.

I am not advocating being aloof and staying out of sight of your people. Being *aloft* is not the same as being *aloof.* I am also not supporting the idea of never interacting with your people on the ground. There is a time and place for all of that to occur (especially if all of the fires are out). I am saying now, as I have said before, that you need to get out of their way so that they can do their jobs. If you are a good forest ranger, then you will know that the best way to do that is to get in your helicopter and get it airborne. Then stay in your helicopter to effectively give support and direction to your firefighters wherever they are in the forest.

I guess my mentors hadn't lost it after all.

Managing Geographically Dispersed Organizations

Today senior managers are increasingly faced with the regionalization and/or globalization of their industries and products, as well as their companies. This geographical dispersion is causing an increase in the number of people who are in remote locations. This may be caused by a planned strategic expansion, pressure from global competition, or as a result of mergers and acquisitions. Regardless of the cause, this condition is real, and, in most cases, the CIO is not immune from its effects. More and more CIOs express the challenges in having to manage people all over the globe. Over one-third of the CIOs that I surveyed indicated that their company had global operations. There is a high probability that they will be managing people in remote locations. I personally managed a large product development organization that spanned three countries. There are obvious challenges with implementing application systems in an organization with many locations, whether they are regional or global. This type of company organizational structure has a way of forcing the IT organization into a similar structure to be effective in its delivery.

So the question becomes, "How do you manage people who are located everywhere?" *Manage the remote people like they are local, and manage the local people like they are remote.* What?

The biggest complaint that I have always heard from *the people* who are remote is that they feel forgotten. Out of sight, out of mind (to use a rather trite, but accurate statement). They also complain that they don't have the same level of access to the management team as the local people. They don't get the opportunity to run into the CIO in the hallway on the way to a meeting. They don't get the chance to poke their heads in your office and ask questions or give updates on an important project. They can't just decide to join you when they see you sitting alone in the company cafeteria or at a local restaurant.

Your local people can.

There are two things you must do. Make it easy for your remote people to have access to you the way the local people do. Also restrict the access that your local people have to you. The latter is obviously very difficult to do. In any case, let's examine the approach.

First, I must begin by saying that I am a strong believer in having an open-door policy. It keeps you informed about progress on key projects. It helps you to stay in touch with situations that would otherwise be outside of your view. Of course, it also helps you keep your finger on the pulse of the progress of your strategic direction. If you have an open-door policy, it is extremely important that you extend it to include your remote staff as well.

Your local people have virtually unrestricted access to you just because they are local. Unfortunately, that access can also have a significant impact on your time and your time management endeavors. Although your people will be able to keep you well informed, they may also prohibit you from getting your helicopter off the ground. In other words, being too available could force you to spend a disproportionate amount of time in a specific area to the detriment of all of the other projects and activities. I am sure you know what I am talking about. It is one or two local individuals who, for whatever reasons, feel it necessary to spend as much time with you as possible. Of course, they will also make sure that your remote team knows that they have a great deal of access to you. This could give the remote people impression that the local projects are more important than the remote projects.

Your remote people could have a number of challenges in addition to their restricted access to you. For example, I had an IT manager in my organization in London, England, who had to double as the landlord in the building in which the team was housed. We were the primary tenants, so that role fell on us. Since my organization was the only one in the building, my senior person there was burdened with the landlord responsibility. There may also be time zone issues, technology maturity issues, phone system issues, language issues, and a whole host of other challenges. These are things that your local people may never encounter. Add these challenges on top of the fact that they cannot access you as often as they would like, and you can see how they could feel a little left out.

I found that the most successful approach was to have a scheduled time for everybody to have access to me. I made it a point to schedule a little more time with the remote people than the local people. For example, my London team was six hours ahead of my time zone. I would come in very early in the morning each day and spend time talking with them on the phone. Everyday I would talk with the manager, and some days (on a predetermined schedule) I would have a telephone meeting with the entire London team. In addition, I budgeted at least a quarterly trip to each remote location and gave them virtually unrestricted access to me while I was there. For the remote offices that were U.S. regional locations, I would schedule monthly visits. I also made sure that I had an office (or at least some space that was designated as my remote office) in each location. This gave them a sense of connection to me. One of my team members once commented that even though they knew that I was thousands of miles away, it was as though I was simply out of the office for a little while. Essentially, it made the remote people feel as though I was local to them.

I also scheduled time with my local team. They knew that regardless of where I was on the planet, on Wednesdays at 10:00 AM we had a meeting. Sometimes the meeting was a video conference, sometimes it was a phone call, and sometimes, if I was in town, it was face-to-face. If the project or the activity that a person was working on at the time had priority over other activities, I would schedule more frequent meetings. I would always treat them as though they were remote even though I may have been the one that was physically remote at the time.

This technique gives balance to your entire team. Manage your remote people like they are local, and manage your local people like they are remote. Your local people don't always have the frequent physical access to you. Your remote team feels like they have an ample amount (and sometimes too much) access to you. In any case, it helps your time management and allows you to keep a focus on all of those important strategic items, regardless of where they are located. It also helps you to stay in the helicopter, even though, in reality, you will probably be in an airplane.

The Main Point—You Can Do It!

I entitled this last chapter "Your People." Of course, that includes you.

I am convinced that the CIO position is one of the most challenging jobs on the planet. In the section entitled, "CIO—'Career is Over,'" you learned that this position is very unique and that the number of people who can truly do this job is small. Now consider one additional fact…you have read this book. That means that you advance yourself through self-development. There are probably a large number of CIOs out there who have not taken the steps that you have. You can be considered the crème de la crème, or the best of the best. You have all of the ingredients to become a very successful CIO. You have the right stuff to be an extremely effective CIO. Researchers and practitioners are generally unable to predict which employees are likely to engage in self-learning activities. I believe I know…the successful ones.

> **What would you recommend to a new CIO as the first thing that they *must* do after assuming their new assignment?**
>
> *"Don't be afraid to make a bold presence. You know your stuff, or you would not have gotten where you are, but don't forget to never stop learning…Learn voraciously…not only IT…but, everything."*
>
> *Linda Pfeiffer, CIO*
> *PC ABC's*

Effective self-development brings together the intellectual power of the mind with effective action in today's complex world. You have begun your journey of effective self-development by reading this book. That can only lead to effective action, which in turn will translate to a successful tenure as CIO. It also means that you truly want to be the best at what you do. You probably also read leadership books, articles and magazines on business, and information on technology trends; attend seminars and tradeshows; and perform any other action that will sharpen your professional skills. Finding the time and discipline to do these things is not easy. That is why many of your colleagues will provide a litany of excuses why they can't and don't do these things. On the flip side, that is why you will do exceptionally well.

You have developed a superior understanding of the CIO position. You have probably also made a mental (or physical) assessment of what you have to do to excel within the position. You know which CIO personalities you will need to engage to make a difference in your company. The challenges of the CIO job are also clearer to you now. That means that you have everything that you need to raise the bar of the CIO position. And that is essentially what your company did when they put *you* there.

It's All about Execution

Does this sound familiar?

I realize that we covered this point earlier; however, I feel like it is one of the most important elements of a CIO's success. You could be good at a lot of things. You could actually be stellar at all of the CIO personalities that we have covered. None of that will mean anything if you do not produce what the company needs when the company needs it in a form that is consistent with the company's strategic direction.

There is a saying, "All activity isn't progress, just like all movement isn't forward." You can have a great deal of activities underway. But are those activities yielding any progress? Are those activities moving you in a direction that will benefit your company and support its goals? As CIO, you must constantly ask yourself these questions. You must constantly ensure that non-productive activities (and processes) are not unnecessarily draining your productivity. Unfortunately, it could be easy for you to do. You are constantly bombarded with new technologies and processes that are going to solve all of your software development problems. It becomes easy for your IT professionals to get so involved in new processes that the focus becomes the *process* rather than the ultimate product that the process is suppose to produce. We hear that complaint from our business partners all the time. Many times they are right. This type of behavior could impact both your ability to bring value to the company as well as your credibility with your business partners. The question from your senior management team becomes, "If the IT department is not bringing value, then why do I need them?"

Peter Drucker once said, "There is nothing quite so useless, as doing with great efficiency, something that should not be done at all." You will need to remove all of those *efficient*, useless processes that are affecting your ability to soundly execute your plans. For every task that is performed, for every project that is underway, for every process that is initiated, and for every meeting that is held, you must determine if it will support the plans and direction you and the company have established. I understand that there are improvements that you may need to make to the IT organization and its processes from time to time. Those things may not appear to be activities that are moving you forward. Those are not the things I am talking about; those items are what we use to call *dues to the future.* Those improvements will help the company in the long run. You will know which items are not moving you forward when you ask the question, "Why are we doing that?" and you are not comfortable with the answer that you receive— or the answer is that they need to get back to you with the answer. Then you should be suspicious of that activity and its impact on your ability to execute.

Remember, its all about execution.

Let's Go for It

My intention was to make this book a mentor to you in your CIO assignment. I am hopeful that I have been successful in that endeavor. Many people talk about this being the first day of the rest of their lives. In your case, this is the first day of the rest of your tenure as CIO. You are now armed with new information, and, hopefully, some new tools and techniques that will help you succeed during that tenure.

You can, and will, make a difference!

You have one of the most important positions within your company because there are very few areas of the company in which you will not be involved. There are very few areas of the company that will not have some dependence on your organization, your decisions, your actions, and your knowledge and skills. You will be expected to participate in the key corporate strategies and then the subsequent execution of those strategies. You will be expected to have knowledge and skills in technology, finance, sales, industry, human resources, marketing, and a whole host of other areas. Each person with whom you interact will have that expectation based on the area from which they came. What is most amazing is that you will develop enough knowledge in each of those areas to be an effective communicator with each of your colleagues. As the CIO, you will have to use the information technology of the company to gain market share, merge or acquire competitors, expand globally, and a myriad of other crucial corporate activities.

Finally, congratulations for becoming one of the most important people in your company. Most of all, I wish you the best of luck in all of your future endeavors.

Now go for it!

Appendix

Chapter

"*It isn't necessary to imagine the world ending in fire or ice-there are two other possibilities: one is paperwork, and the other is nostalgia.*"
—Frank Zappa (1940–1993)

Knowledge Nuggets

As I previously mentioned, in researching this book I consulted with a large number of current CIOs. Many of them were kind enough to provide a great deal of wisdom about the position that can only be acquired through experience, what I call "knowledge nuggets." I call them nuggets because to me they are as valuable as the gold nuggets that were mined by the Forty-niners many years ago. In my opinion, that makes this section one of the most valuable sections in the book. I want this book to be a mentor to CIOs. Well, this is the section where the *real* mentoring takes place. This is the place where you get the opportunity to truly benefit from the knowledge and skill that professionals who are performing this job have to share.

Knowledge Nugget #1

Your first nugget will come from me. I previously mentioned that I had some very good mentors early in my career. One such mentor was Rod. I worked for Rod over thirty years ago. In our manufacturing company, Rod was the vice president of data processing (the title CIO had not yet been invented). Rod gave me a bit of advice once that I never forgot. It is important to mention that I received this nugget right after I had made a decision that essentially ruined the accounting books of the majority of the divisions within our company. Our company, at the time, had earnings of over $1.4 billion. The details of the bad decision are unimportant. The lesson about how to make decisions was very important.

Rod called me (and my director) into his office the day after I made that notoriously bad decision. He asked me, among other things, if I had been 100 percent sure about my decision at the time that I had made it. I found it extremely difficult to answer the question. I think it was partly because I was convinced that he was about the fire me—partly because I had never been called into the vice president's office before for making a mistake and partly because I don't think I was 100 percent sure at the time. In any case, after a very long pause, Rod said to me, *"Always be 100 percent sure of 50 percent of your decisions."* He then told me that I was to meet with him the next morning and explain to him what he just said to me. I dutifully left his office, relieved by the fact that, since I had to be back in the morning, at least I would be working there one more day!

The next morning, I met with Rod very early. I told him that I had completely understood his message. What he was telling me was that if I was 100 percent sure of 50 percent of my decisions, then half of the time I would be dead right.

Assuming I had a fifty-fifty chance of being right on the other 50 percent, on average I would be dead right 75 percent of the time. Rod told me that I was correct and praised me on my reasoning ability. He then proceeded to tell me that on the final 25 percent, which of course would probably not be good decisions, to just be sure that they were little things! I never forgot those words. Since then, I have made a number of less-than-stellar decisions. Fortunately, they were mostly little things.

By the way, I did gather up the courage to ask Rod why he didn't fire me. He told me that my mistake had cost the company nearly a million dollars to fix. He also said that he was convinced that I would never make a mistake like that again. Therefore, he did not understand why he should fire me when he had just invested close to a million dollars on my education! He told me to go back to work and that he was 100 percent sure about his decision.

Knowledge Nugget #2

Always know there is someone out there who can do the job better than you. Learn to balance your time between family, business, and having fun. Always remember that no matter what, put your family first, because if you don't have a peaceful life at home, it will affect everything else!

Patrick O'Neal
Griffin and O'Neal Staffing

Knowledge Nugget #3

Identify key staff and learn what and how they do things. Identify key peers and learn what and how they do things. Make sure that you are able to deliver on all requests and become a valuable resource to your company.

Howard Moskowitz
Ann Arbor Public Schools

Knowledge Nugget #4

Understand the business; understand the business' goals; and understand their pain. Don't overlook business process. If the process is flawed, the systems just make a flawed process generate more flaws…which usually costs you money.

Rob Adams
Twin Modal, Inc

Knowledge Nugget #5

Fully disclose all of IT projects, resources, and capacity. Let all senior managers know what you are working on and how it affects them. I manage resources no differently than a warehouse or production line. Mine are just more mysterious, and you need to remove that mystery.

Mike Anderson
Cosmetic Essence, Inc.

Knowledge Nugget #6

Choose your words carefully. There are often people who will misinterpret one sentence, and it becomes fact throughout the organization. Know your audience well before making any flippant remarks.

Vince Sheehan
Indiana University School of Medicine

Knowledge Nugget #7

It is important for a new CIO to understand that there are three essential skill sets required to lead a successful IT department. They are people, business, and technology skills, in that order. Every IT leader must stay in touch with the people that their organization supports. Even the most elegant solution to address the business and technical needs of a project will fail if the needs and concerns of the people who use the system are not properly addressed.

Dennis Milks
Weld Racing

Knowledge Nugget #8

Don't jump the gun on ROI on a project. Make sure the numbers are accurate.

Stuart Blair
Daily News-Sun

Knowledge Nugget #9

Read *everything*!

Linda Pfeiffer
PC ABC's

Knowledge Nugget #10

You can't just force something to happen; it works much better to gain buy-in and consensus (at all levels within the organization—inside and outside IT).

Ron Ehlers

Knowledge Nugget #11

Most existing technologies within the company are either too costly, inefficient, redundant, or simply outdated. The challenge is to get buy-in to replace or upgrade older systems with new, perhaps initially costlier technologies, but that will, in the long run, translate into great ROI. Therefore, good relations with the CEO and CFO are crucial.

Suzanne Tonini, CIO
MTR, Inc.

Sample Job Descriptions

I thought it might be helpful for you to see a couple of different CIO job descriptions. These descriptions were given to me by people who currently hold these positions. It may give you some ideas for your own job description. I have removed references to any specific company.

After reading these job descriptions, you will notice that, regardless of the industry, the primary functions of the CIO are the same. Companies need a CIO who is technically savvy while at the same time strategically focused. Think of the multiple personalities presented in chapter 3 and then reread these job descriptions. I think you will agree that many of the personalities discussed can be found within these descriptions.

LARGE TECHNOLOGY COMPANY

Reporting to president and CEO of the business sector, and with a dotted line reporting relationship to the company's chief information officer, the sector CIO will serve as the principal information technology advisor for the sector leadership team and have management responsibility for a global organization comprised of over 250 professionals plus additional shared resources. Near-term deliverables include fully integrating the recently implemented order-to-cash system into all frontline business activities and partnering with the Corporate Information Systems organization to capture future benefits associated with the ongoing shift from a product-centric business model to a software and service-driven sector—including the development of more robust management information systems. He or she will also have primary responsibility for leading the sector's IT activities by doing the following:

- Developing a robust understanding of the sector's strategies and the resultant IT needs. Assess the current IT systems in place and develop, implement, and evolve the tactical and strategic IT plans for the sector.
- Creating a seamless and integrated fact-based management decision system through which the senior leadership team will be able to more effectively direct the sector business strategies and plans.
- Identifying the need for designing, coordinating, implementing, and evaluating the effectiveness of the sector's IT policies, procedures, and systems

to ensure effective and cost-efficient information resources to support and advance the sector's strategic and tactical objectives.

- Conceptualizing, designing, testing, implementing, and evaluating IT systems and applications.

- Becoming a valued member of the sector's executive team through participation in the strategy-setting meetings and discussions. Interfacing with senior management to effectively translate and implement IT needs across the organization.

- Envisioning and realizing the optimum utility of IT by assisting senior leaders in recognizing where new technology would enhance performance while transforming or supporting program operations.

- Identifying and arranging to fulfill all requirements for IT support activities to ensure that the sector's investment in IT achieves its potential.

- Integrating and leveraging IT assets across the company to provide shared products and services in a seamless fashion to the customer.

- Developing and enhancing the systems plan to provide strong cross-functional relationships throughout the company.

- Building and managing a team of experienced, talented IT professionals, including motivating, training, recruitment, retention, and career development.

This high-profile position will represent the sector's IT functions to the industry, government, and association and community groups. It will maintain market intelligence to identify and leverage opportunities as it relates to IT. This will include current and future opportunities in addition to developing new products and relationships, which will continue to maintain the competitive advantage.

SOFTWARE DEVELOPMENT COMPANY

The chief information officer will hold overall management responsibility for the company's applications development, database management, network and communication services, and end-user computing functions. This position influences the management committee and provides input to corporate-wide decisions. The CIO is involved with and influences prospects, customers, and the internal sales cycle. Frequently, the individual in this position is the voice of the company to the outside community.

This position entails leading a geographically dispersed organization of more than one hundred thirty information technology professionals in ten countries. The chief information officer's management oversight will also include operating four data centers and a global network that services approximately thirty locations and supports more than twenty-five hundred worldwide employees, nine thousand customers, and six hundred business partners.

Key Relationships

Reports to: Chief financial officer

Direct Reports: Four directors for applications service, end-user com-
                           puting, business performance management systems,
                           and network and communications services

Other Key Relationships:

   Internal:

        • Senior management team members, including the CEO and
          board of directors, as well as the company's worldwide end-user
          community.

   External:

        • Technology vendors
        • Business partners
        • Industry analysts
        • Prospects and customers

Responsibilities include the following:

        • Develop and manage the global IT organization.
        • Provide strategic direction and oversight in the following areas:

        1   Corporate applications systems—selection, integration, and
            support of packaged applications; database administration
            and management; and business process re-engineering.

2　　Business performance management systems—development and support of company's data warehouse, query and reporting, OLAP, financial analytic applications, customer/market analytic applications, scorecards, and dashboards.

3　　Network and communications services—provisioning and operation of the company's data centers and voice and data networks.

4　　End-user computing—support for the worldwide mobile workforce of sales and consultants and development and support of laptop and Web-based product demonstration environments.

- Establish effective partnerships and working relationships with entire senior management team on a global basis.
- Act as one of the principal technology advisors to the management committee regarding the present and future uses of technology as a strategic competitive weapon, and guide senior management's understanding and effective sponsorship of IT initiatives.
- Develop, execute, and manage a vision for rolling out company products within the organization.
- Effectively represent the company to the high-tech community.
- Support corporate business development and strategic planning initiatives.
- Demonstrate exemplary abilities in strategic planning and overall business acumen.
- Quickly learn and become a key internal knowledge resource for the company's products, positioning, and customer base.
- Position the chief information officer at the front end of evaluating and planning for potential acquisitions.
- Represent the company at customer and partner events.
- Improve processes for efficiency.
- Manage an annual budget of approximately $25 million and serve as a member of the capital expenditure committee.

MAJOR INSURANCE COMPANY

The chief information officer (CIO) of the Advisor's Division reports directly to the CIO of the company in the United States. He/she has an indirect and matrix-reporting relationship to the Advisor's Division's COO. The CIO is the senior solutions executive responsible for the direction of systems and technologies for the company Advisor's Division and across its eight nationwide broker/dealers. The CIO provides vision, architecture, and business-driven technical strategies at an enterprise level and operates as a key management team member for the business.

This CIO leads the Advisor's Division technology team and ensures his/her team delivers reliable, value-added business solutions in a cost-effective and timely manner. Additionally, the CIO is responsible for rationalizing the value of the existing IT landscape, as well as providing the technology thought leadership for appropriate solutions moving forward that will enable the business to meet its strategic growth objectives. These areas include, but are not be limited to, technology architecture, applications development, package solutions evaluation and selection, operations delivery, and project management, along with creating an effective model for capital project funding and IT governance priority with the business.

The CIO works closely with eight broker/dealer presidents to ensure he/she understands the major technology needs and initiatives, including the following:

- Review, approve, and prioritize all major technology purchases, development projects, and system implementation initiatives, ensuring business value-added emphasis.
- Provide architectural and plan reviews for all systems implementations throughout each project's life cycle.
- Identify projects that will be leveraged at a network enterprise level and/or completed with network resources.
- Direct decision-making authority on project approval, design, and implementation timelines.
- Review and ensure all technology-related contracts within company Advisor's Division and affiliated broker/dealers go through the company's appropriate legal and strategic sourcing channels.

Responsibilities include the following:

- Create technology vision and definition of the future platforms required to support the company Advisor's Division, ensuring the technology infrastructure enhances the company's clients' interactions with suppliers and customers.
- Provide expert-level technology consulting to Advisor's Division and each of the broker/dealers to facilitate technology decision-making.

- Contribute and provide thought leadership to the long-range business planning processes and assurance that investments in technical solutions, architecture, and tools are closely aligned with company's U.S. IT and business objectives.
- Identify and leverage enterprise solution opportunities across Advisor's Division, the network broker/dealers, and the U.S. company.
- Develop and manage external service provider relationships and involvement in technology contractual agreements for the delivery of technical products and services in conjunction with company strategic sourcing.
- Provide motivation, leadership, and people development of the technical staff across Advisor's Division.
- Establish and rationalize the division's multimillion dollar IT budget and project plan and management of initiatives to ensure satisfactory adherence to both.
- Identify and manage strategic division-level IT initiatives to deliver functionality that will significantly impact the business, improving operational efficiencies, access to information, and competitive advantage.

Serve as liaison between the company's U.S. IT, company Advisor's Division, and the company broker/dealer firms to ensure the network understands the overall company technical direction and standards. Ensure network issues and considerations are raised and are part of the company's corporate technical decision-making process.

BUSINESS SERVICES COMPANY

The chief information officer (CIO) reports to the president and CEO. The company has sales of $250 million and 2,000 employees. The business provides electronic payment solutions to providers and customers engaged in commerce, any time, any place. It helps financial services customers and retailers manage, secure, and process debit-related transactions while minimizing risk and optimizing customer opportunity. End-to-end solutions include customer and identity verification, transaction authorization, capture, conversion, processing, and settlement. The company's six businesses each lead in their respective markets. The projected growth of the company is 20 percent per year, and year-to-date it is ahead of projection.

The scope of the CIO position includes the business's technology, including internal information systems (hardware and software), customer products, telecommunications, and Web-enabled products. The direct reports of the CIO include directors of: data centers, networks, call centers, installation/conversion, outsourcing, and information technology development. In total, the function has approximately 1,000 employees with a budget approaching $150 million.

Responsibilities include the following:

- Leading the company effort to bring current knowledge, best practices, and a future vision of technology, which will enhance competitive position, meet business goals, reduce operating costs, and increase user efficiency.
- Understanding and recognizing changes and trends in information technology, and interpreting their impact on the business.
- Determining the long-term corporate-wide information needs, and developing a strategy to address those needs, including systems development, hardware acquisition, and integration of mainframe and client/server applications.
- Providing the highest level of support with the product, market, and business development functions in determining the overall information systems approaches and priorities.
- Assuring the integrity of corporate data, proprietary information, and related intellectual property through information security and access management.
- Integrating the information technology functions of newly acquired companies in a timely manner.

The challenges of this position are as follows:

- Leading the successful technology integration of six newly combined businesses in both infrastructure and people. This includes consolidating call centers and data centers.
- Aligning the employees and using their skills to achieve a cohesive team environment.
- Creating the future vision for information technology as a competitive weapon.
- Providing coordination with the other functional areas to achieve established objectives with technology and information.

FINANCIAL SERVICES COMPANY

Provide overall direction and management of the information technology operational groups. Responsibilities include overseeing the system maintenance and development function of the IT infrastructure, partnering with executive management of the five operational areas in formulating and optimizing the strategic goals and objectives for the corporation, and being at the forefront of driving change and improvement in the company's overall IT performance.

Responsibilities include the following:

- Work with existing team to establish a comprehensive strategy for new application development and the migration of existing applications.
- Implement and execute an IT vision to support overall strategic plan for the business group.
- Create an environment where IT involvement and consultation is central to business workflow for technology-related initiatives.
- Ensure that the work done throughout the various technical disciplines is reviewed from a strategic perspective and that it is aligned with tactical and corporate-level goals.
- Provide overall strategic direction to the business relationship team to enhance the level of service to different brands and shared service departments.
- Enhance the operational effectiveness of corporate programs as they pertain to technology.
- Ensure the use of service-level agreements to support IT performance.
- Work in collaboration with the business group senior leadership to implement best practices throughout IT. Will ensure a consistent total quality approach to deliver on-time, on-budget, on-quality applications and IT services.
- Provide a functionally rich, cost-effective, Internet-based operating platform for all brands, brokers, and agents.
- Guide and assist all company brands in the effective use of technology to market and manage franchise operations and franchisee's

services by creating successful deployment strategies that take full advantage of customer insights.

- Leverage Internet technologies to create an environment of single point of data entry and seamless information flow.

- Ensure that the requirements of each IT and business area receiving services through and affected by the outsourcing relationships are met effectively and efficiently.

- Anticipate technology and/or market trends and provide guidance on their application to external customers and feedback of business requirements.

- Drive department value through consistent delivery.

- Manage a multimillion dollar annual budget, including developing and maintaining the annual operating and capital budgets for the company information and technology systems operations.

- Make focused decisions pertaining to building vs. buying, relative to outsourcing and in-house provisioning of IT services and skills.

- Manage, develop, and grow a team of 35+ employees.

MANUFACTURING COMPANY

The chief information officer (CIO) is charged with the proactive creation and implementation of comprehensive technology plans. The CIO must be a strategic thought leader who is on the cutting edge of technology. The CIO must have the ability to drive the company into the future. The responsibilities include data and telecommunications systems, Internet and intranet initiatives, systems consolidation, rationalization, design and re-architecture, and connectivity projects designed to fully support the attainment of company growth strategies.

The plans that are developed must effectively leverage information technology to drive significant competitive advantage and differentiation as well as cost effectiveness. The CIO is expected to spend significant time with the business and product line leaders and be held accountable for ensuring an acceptable level of return on all IT investments.

Responsibilities include the following:

- Fuse technology and business strategies to ensure the development and execution of a technology plan that supports individual product lines.
- Mentor and evaluate employees for building/maintaining a strong team.
- Identify and evaluate new enabling technologies and architectural platforms relevant to supporting the business.
- Monitor emerging technology trends on an ongoing basis to meet existing and future business requirements.
- Cultivate effective relationships with vendors and other business partners required to maintain leadership for the company.
- Work closely with other members of the senior management team to ensure the proper alignment of business systems and technology strategies, plans, and priorities.
- Provide leadership and personal direction to staff, challenging them to achieve at the highest levels while creating a positive and constructive team environment.
- Identify solution sets for business opportunities through a strong technology team with strong business applications expertise.
- Develop the information systems staffing plan for future operations, balancing the use of external and internal resources.
- Participate in merger and acquisition activity associated with the business, including, but not limited to, due diligences in the technology components of an acquisition.
- Act as lead technology consultant with the line of business.

As CIO, you must be able to complete the following:

- Build, lead, and motivate a team
- Plan and execute an IT strategy
- Negotiate strategic alliances
- Project a vision
- Be creative

- Partner with the business line leader
- Manage both upward and downward
- Operate effectively within a fast-paced environment
- Develop and deliver effective oral and written presentations
- Influence others
- Mentor employees
- Fuse business and technology
- Be able to multitask, managing multiple projects simultaneously

Glossary & Acronyms

Chapter **7**

"Things should be made as simple as possible, but no simpler."
—Albert Einstein

Glossary

The path to the CIO position is not the same for everyone. As a result, many times the people within the CIO organization may use words, terms, and acronyms that are not familiar to every CIO. For example, a CIO who has progressed through the applications development career path may not be familiar with network terminology; CIOs who came up through the infrastructure or data center ranks may not be used to the terms used in the data modeling area, and so forth. Therefore, I have included a glossary of terms that are commonly used in different areas of IT. This is not an exhaustive list; however, it should help any CIO who may not have experienced all areas of IT during their journey to the CIO position.

A

Active Directory

A Microsoft technology based on the Lightweight Directory Access Protocol (LDAP) that provides a unified view and way to manage all objects on a network. The directory service portion of the Windows 2000 operating system. Active Directory manages the identities and relationships of the distributed resources that make up a network environment. It stores information about network-based entities (such as applications, files, printers, and people) and provides a consistent way to name, describe, locate, access, manage, and secure information about these resources.

Active Server Pages (ASP)

Technology that generates HTML and passes the dynamically created HTML to the Web browser to be displayed to the end user. It is designed to allow combinations of HTML, scripts (such as JavaScript and Microsoft's VBScript), and ActiveX to easily be used. ASP automatically senses whether the user's browser supports ActiveX. If it does, an applet is downloaded. If the browser does not, ASP runs the applet on the server and broadcasts the result to the user on the client computer.

Advanced Interactive eXecutive (AIX)	IBM's version of UNIX. An open operating system based on UNIX technology. IBM produces a version of AIX for its RS/6000 hardware.
Advanced Peer-to-Peer Networking (APPN)	Technology that enables computers to dynamically exchange information, making it simpler to configure and maintain SNA networks. An extension of IBM's Systems Network Architecture (SNA) that provides dynamic, multipath routing among computers in an SNA network. The original hierarchical SNA network structure inhibited any-to-any connectivity. APPN addressed this issue.
American National Standards Institute (ANSI)	The American National Standards Institute (ANSI) is a private, nonprofit organization that administers and coordinates the U.S. voluntary standardization and conformity assessment system.
American Standard Code for Information Interchange (ASCII)	A code with seven information signals plus one parity check signal, designed for interworking between computers (i.e., the transmittal of text). It is a character encoding based on the English alphabet. The numeric codes represent text in computers, communications equipment, and other devices that work with text. Most computers use ASCII numerical codes to represent text, which makes it possible to transfer data from one computer to another. The following table describes the ASCII code and the corresponding character:

ASCII	CHARACTER	ASCII	CHARACTER	ASCII	CHARACTER
0	NUL – null	61	=	122	z
1	SOH – start of heading	62	>	123	{
2	STX – start of text	63	?	124		
3	ETX – end of text	64	@	125	}
4	EOT – end of transmission	65	A	126	~
5	ENQ – enquiry	66	B	127	DEL – delete
6	ACK – acknowledge	67	C	128	Ç
7	BEL – bell	68	D	129	ü
8	BS – backspace	69	E	130	é
9	TAB – horizontal tab	70	F	131	â
10	LF – NL line feed, new line	71	G	132	ä

11	VT – vertical tab	72	H	133	à
12	FF – NP form feed, new page	73	I	134	â
13	CR – carriage return	74	J	135	ç
14	SO – shift out	75	K	136	ê
15	SI – shift in	76	L	137	ë
16	DLE – data line escape	77	M	138	è
17	DC1 – device control 1 – XON	78	N	139	ï
18	DC2 – device control 2	79	O	140	î
19	DC3 – device control 3 – XOFF	80	P	141	ì
20	DC4 – device control 4	81	Q	142	Ä
21	NAK – negative acknowledge	82	R	143	Å
22	SYN – synchronous idle	83	S	144	É
23	ETB – end of transmission block	84	T	145	æ
24	CAN – cancel	85	U	146	Æ
25	EM – end of medium	86	V	147	ô
26	SUB – substitute	87	W	148	ö
27	ESC – escape	88	X	149	ò
28	FS – file separator	89	Y	150	û
29	GS – group separator	90	Z	151	ù
30	RS – record separator	91	[	152	ÿ
31	US – unit separator	92	\	153	Ö
32	SPACE	93	]	154	Ü
33	!	94	^	155	¢
34	"	95	_	156	£
35	#	96	`	157	¥
36	$	97	a	158	P
37	%	98	b	159	ƒ
38	&	99	c	160	á
39	'	100	d	161	í
40	(	101	e	162	ó
41	)	102	f	163	ú
42	*	103	g	164	ñ
43	+	104	h	165	Ñ
44	,	105	i	166	ª
45	-	106	j	167	º
46	.	107	k	168	¿
47	/	108	l	169	⌐
48	0	109	m	170	¬
49	1	110	n	171	½
50	2	111	o	172	¼
51	3	112	p	173	¡
52	4	113	q	174	«
53	5	114	r	175	»
54	6	115	s		
55	7	116	t		
56	8	117	u		
57	9	118	v		

58	:		119	w
59	;		120	x
60	<		121	y

Andrew File System (AFS) A system that allots users a potion of space on a server and allows them to share files. It requires special software to access but may also be accessed through a Web portal. It is a distributed network file system that enables files from any AFS machine across the country to be accessed as easily as files stored locally. It is composed of cells. Each cell represents an independently administered portion of file space. Cells connect to form one enormous file system under the root directory.

Applications Program Interface (API) An API allows a developer to program a pre-constructed interface (the API) instead of programming directly to a device or piece of software. It allows the developer to write programs without having to have an in-depth knowledge of the device or software to which they are sending the commands.

Application Service Provider (ASP) A company that runs a software application on its computers and allows other organizations and/or individuals to use that application. An ASP often provides this service through the Internet on some form of fee-for-service basis. The application service provider typically provides all hardware, software, maintenance, support, and other services needed to run the application.

Artifact An artifact is a piece of information that is created, modified, or used by a process such as a model, use case, document, source code, or executable file.

Artificial Intelligence (AI) The capability of a computer to perform functions that are normally associated with human intelligence, such as reasoning, learning, or self-improvement. It is a set of disciplines within computer science that attempts to make computers become intelligent by enabling them to use processes similar to those used by the human brain.

Asymmetrical Digital Subscriber Line (ADSL)	A protocol for providing high rates of data delivery (6–9 Mbps) over existing copper phone lines.
Asymmetric Cryptography	A cryptographic system in which encryption and decryption are performed using different keys.
Asynchronous Transfer Mode (ATM)	A networking protocol initially designed to move multimedia data around with high reliability and speed. It is a network technology for both local and wide area networks (LANs and WANs) that supports data, video, and real-time voice. The technology uses switches that establish a logical circuit from end to end. The idle bandwidth in ATMs can be reallocated and used when needed, unlike telephone switches that dedicate the circuits.
Automatic Call Distributor (ACD)	A phone system that can handle many incoming calls. The major advantage of automatic call distributors is that they are designed to distribute a large volume of incoming calls uniformly across multiple operators or agents.

B

Backbone	The main segment of a network to which all other segments are connected. It links several workgroup LANs together in a single building or several networks together in a campus or MAN environment. It is usually a high-speed transmission facility, or an arrangement of such facilities, designed to interconnect lower-speed distribution channels or clusters of dispersed user devices. All systems with connectivity to the backbone have connectivity to one another. Systems can set up private connections that bypass the backbone for reasons of cost, performance, or security.

Bandwidth	The capacity of a network or data connection to transmit data. The range of frequencies that can pass over a given transmission channel. The bandwidth determines the rate at which information can be transmitted through the circuit. The greater the bandwidth, the more information that can be sent in a given amount of time. Analog transmission usually expressed in kHz or MHz, digital transmission, bps or Mbps. Fiber-optic bandwidth is usually given as its capacity to transmit information in a specific time period for a specific length. On average, typical telephone lines can carry 1K of information per second.
Baud Rate	A unit of measurement that denotes the number of bits that can be transmitted per second. For example, if a modem is rated at 9600 baud it can transmit data at a rate of 9,600 bits per second (bps). The term was derived from the name of J. M. E. Baudot, a French pioneer in printing telegraphy. Transmission speeds are now more commonly measured bits per second (bps) rather than bauds.
Bluetooth	A wireless networking technology. It has a range of about ten meters and a raw data transmission rate of one megabit per second. It is a standard for cable-free connectivity between mobile phones, mobile PCs, handheld computers, and other peripherals. It is an initiative that was started by Ericsson, IBM, Intel, Nokia, and Toshiba to establish the standard. The term *Bluetooth* comes from a Scandinavian king who first federated the Scandinavian countries. The king had a dark broken tooth.
Business Process Modeling (BPM)	It is an activity performed by business analysts to model both the current state of an enterprise and the intended future state. It is likely that IT systems development will be required to transition from the current state to the future state. However, IT sys-

tems development is not always a requirement. Sometimes the establishment, modification, or elimination of a manual process could accomplish the goal.

Business Process Modeling Language (BPML)

A modeling language for business processes. It is a language designed to document a business system using a combination of text and graphical notation. It is a tool used by business analyst when performing business process modeling on an organization.

C

Capability Maturity Model (CMM)

CMM is a method developed by Software Engineering Institute (SEI) for evaluating and measuring the maturity of the software development process of organizations. There are five maturity levels, each a layer in the foundation for ongoing process improvement, designated by the numbers 1 through 5. Level 1 is the Initial stage; Level 2 is the managed (or repeatable) stage; Level 3 is the defined stage; Level 4 is the quantitatively managed stage; and Level 5 is the optimization stage.

Level 1 Ad Hoc — No development methodology exists and few, if any, controls are in place. It is difficult to determine if progress is being made since there is a lack of measurement.

Level 2 Repeatable — A set of tasks and processes has been defined well enough to forecast project results with reasonable accuracy. However, no method for forecasting improvements or making trade-offs has been implemented.

Level 3 Defined   A development process is implemented and understood, measurements are taken, and the process is predictable enough to anticipate the effect of implementing new technologies.

Level 4 Managed   A considerable amount of quantitative and qualitative improvements are likely. This is because the process is managed and evolutionary. Each technology implementation is part of an overall architecture.

Level 5 Optimized   A level in the development organization where the environment drives the process. The primary activity at this level is focused on improving the process rather than executing it.

Capital Costs   Typically, those cost applying to the physical (substantial) assets of the organization. Traditionally those assets were the accommodation and machinery necessary to produce the enterprises product. Capital costs are the purchase or major enhancement of fixed assets (i.e., building and plant). An example would be computer hardware. These costs are often referred to as one-off costs.

Cellular Digital Packet Data (CDPD)   An Internet Protocol (IP)-based network technology that allows cellular providers to offer remote and mobile computing by transmitting digital data over their networks. It uses unused bandwidth normally used by mobile phones between 800 and 900 MHz to transfer data. During 2004, many major carriers in the United States threatened to shut down CDPD service. Today, many have done so.

Control Objectives for Information and related Technology (COBIT)	COBIT is an IT governance framework (best practices) and supporting toolset that allows managers to close the gap between business needs, risks, control, and security through the improvement of safeguards and controls throughout the IT process. In 1992, it was created by the Information Systems Audit and Control Association (ISACA), and the IT Governance Institute (ITGI).
Code Division Multiple Access (CDMA)	A second-generation digital wireless technology that allows multiple calls to share a radio frequency in the 800MHz–1.9GHz band without causing interference. It is a method of multiple accesses that encodes data with a particular code associated with a channel. It provides for the simultaneous transmission and reception of several messages, each of which has a coded identity to distinguish it from the other messages. It does not divide up the channel by time (as in TDMA), or frequency (as in FDMA). It uses the constructive interference properties of the signal medium to perform the multiplexing.
Color Graphics Adapter (CGA)	It is a color video format for computer display monitors. It was introduced by IBM in the early 1980s. It was the first color computer display standard for the IBM PC. The equipment provides 200 × 600 pixel resolution for digital (rather than analog) video signals.
Common Development Environment (CDE)	It is a proprietary desktop environment for UNIX. It is based on Motif (a graphical user interface toolkit) and was developed by the Common Open Software Environment (COSE) group. It was the first user interface specification from a consortium of major vendors (i.e., Hewlett-Packard, IBM, Novell, and Sun Microsystems) that was dedicated to standardizing Unix. This consortium no longer

exists. It is also the standard desktop environment on HP OpenVMS.

Common Gateway Interface (CGI)	It is a set of rules that describe how a Web server communicates with another piece of software on the same machine and how the other piece of software (the CGI program) talks to the Web server. It is a data-passing specification used when a Web server must send or receive data from an application such as a database. It is a program that is executed by the HTTP server whenever the client clicks on some element in a Web page.
Common Object Request Broker (CORBA)	It is a specification created by the Object Management Group (OMG) for distributed, scalable components. It is a standard that allows programs or objects to communicate, even though they may have been written in different environments by different vendors. The architecture is a collection of objects and libraries that allow the creation of applications in a distributed environment to contain objects that make and receive requests and responses.
Configuration Item (CI)	Component of an infrastructure or an item, such as a request for change, associated with an infrastructure which is (or is to be) under the control of configuration management. CIs may vary widely in complexity, size, and type, from an entire system (including all hardware, software, and documentation) to a single module or a minor hardware component.
Configuration Management	The process of identifying and defining the configuration items in a system, recording and reporting the status of configuration items and requests for change, and verifying the completeness and correctness of configuration items.

Critical Success Factors (CFS)	A measure of success or maturity of a project or process. It can be a state, a deliverable, or a milestone. An example of an IT CSF would be completing the production of an overall technology strategy.
Customer Information & Control System (CICS)	It is a general-purpose online transaction-processing (OLTP) subsystem for implementing transaction-processing applications. It was created by IBM and runs primarily on IBM mainframes. It is a transaction-processing system designed for both the online and batch-processing environments. Currently, there are versions of CICS that are also available for UNIX and other platforms.

D

Data Definition Language (DDL)	It is a computer language for defining data. It is used to describe the data model for a Structured Query Language (SQL) database. It describes such things as the names and access paths for the data. In addition, it describes how the various data components are interrelated. It also illustrates in what general form the data appears as well as the fields that define the data.
Data Warehousing	A collection of data gathered and organized so that it can easily be analyzed, extracted, synthesized, and otherwise used for further understanding of the data.
Demilitarized Zone (DMZ)	It is the name given to the protected area between an enterprise's computer systems and the public Internet. This is the subnet that exists between two firewalls. One firewall is in front of the public Internet, and the second firewall is in front of the protected enterprise machines. The servers that reside in the DMZ determine the access permission of the Internet traffic. The following is a picture of a typical network DMZ design:

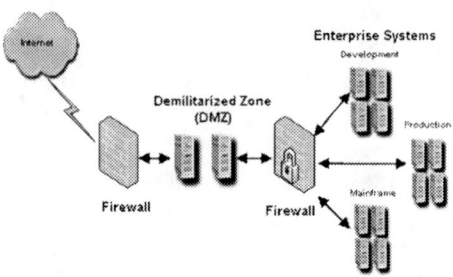

Figure 11. Example of a DMZ (demilitarized zone).

Denial of Service Attack

A security attack on a network that floods it with so many requests that regular traffic is either slowed or completely interrupted. It is a deliberate attempt to disable a network. It starts with an innocent ping utility to determine whether a specific IP address is accessible.

Digital Subscriber
Line (DSL)

A technology that is a local phone company's response to the speed of cable modems. It is a group of technologies that provide digital data transmission over copper wires. Typically, the download speed of DSL ranges from 128 Kbs to 6000 Kbs depending on DSL technology and service level implemented. It can be synchronous (SDSL) or asynchronous (ADSL). Upload speeds are lower than download speeds for ADSL and the same for SDSL.

Distributed Computing
Environment (DCE)

An industry-standard, vendor-neutral set of distributed computing technologies. A computing environment in which data and applications are distributed among dissimilar computers. The computers are linked and integrated in such a way that they function as a single environment. Some vendors have developed tools (which they call DCE) for developing and deploying enterprise-wide applications in a distributed computing environment.

Distributed File System (DFS)	A technology that allows multiple servers and shared directories on a network to appear as a single network drive. It is a file system that supports sharing of files and resources in the form of persistent storage over a network. It enables the centralization of network file system resources into a single logical location.
Distributed Management Environment (DME)	A set of network management specifications defined by the Open Software Foundation (OSF, which is now called the Open Systems Group). In addition, it is a network monitoring and control protocol. It represents a structure under which the management of systems and networks can be brought together. The following is an example of the DME framework:

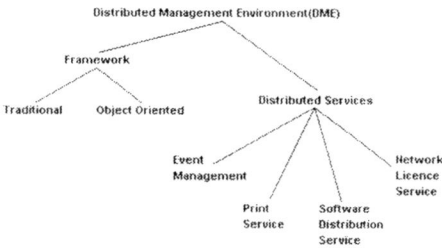

Figure 12. Example of Distributed Management Environment (DME) framework.

Domain Naming Service (DNS)	A system or network service that stores information associated with domain names in a distributed database on IP networks like the Internet. It serves as the map between the logical names (i.e., the text names as we see them) and the network addresses (i.e., the numbers that a computer can recognize) in the network. In an address on the Internet, the domain name is the segment just after "http://." This is also known as the Uniform Resource Locator (URL).

Dynamic Data Exchange (DDE)	A method of exchanging data between dissimilar applications. It is an older technology that is similar to OLE (see "Object Linking and Imbedding"). It enables multiple applications to have access to the same data. For example, a word-processing application can exchange data with a spreadsheet application. OLE provides a more sophisticated approach to the technology of sharing data between applications.
Dynamic HTML (DHTML)	A technology that has client-side methods for enhancing the capabilities of Web browsers and HTML documents. It enables the developers to dynamically change the rendering and content of a document without being concerned with server-side applications. It is a method of creating interactive Web sites by using a combination of a static markup language HTML, a client-side scripting language (such as JavaScript), and the presentation definition language Cascading Style Sheets (i.e., the language used to describe the presentation of a document written in a markup language).
Dynamic Link Library (DLL)	A Windows mechanism that links executable code modules to an application program or process. It is Microsoft's implementation of the shared library concept in the Windows operating system environment.
Dynamic Host Configuration Protocol (DHCP)	A client-server networking protocol. It is a protocol for assigning dynamic Internet Protocol (IP) addresses to devices on a network to newly attached clients. A DHCP server is used to assign a TCP/IP address from a pool of TCP/IP addresses to a client that supports DHCP. In some systems, the device's IP address can even change while it is still connected. It enables address pooling and allocation, and simplifies TCP/IP installation and administration.

E

Electronic Business XML (ebXML)

It is a framework that provides a dictionary of com mon business objects (such as names, postal addresses, etc.) and a prevailing protocol for communicating transactions. It is a family of XML-based standards sponsored by the Organization for the Advancement of Structured Information Standards (OASIS) and the United Nations Center for Trade Facilitation and Electronic Business (UN/CEFACT), whose mission is to provide an open, XML-based infrastructure that enables the global use of electronic business information in an interoperable, secure, and consistent manner by all trading partners.

Electronic Data Interchange (EDI)

It is the computer-to-computer exchange of structured information by agreed message standards from one computer application to another by electronic means. It is the data format used by the vast majority of electronic commerce transactions in the world.

Enhanced Graphics Array (EGA)

A graphics standard that allows resolutions up to 640×350 pixels and sixteen colors from a palette of sixty-four. It is an IBM PC computer display standard specification located between the Color Graphics Adapter (CGA) and the Video Graphics Array (VGA) in graphics performance (i.e., color and space resolution).

Enterprise Resource Planning (ERP)

It is a class of software designed to help organizations plan and organize business functions. It is an information system that automates many of the business practices related to the operations and/or production functions of a company. It is software that integrates manufacturing, financial, and distribution functions to balance and optimize enterprise resources. The software generally includes integrated manufacturing, distribution, and financial applications.

Extensible Markup Language (XML)	It is a standard that was approved as a World Wide Web Consortium (W3C) recommendation. It is a general-purpose markup language for creating special-purpose markup languages, capable of describing many different kinds of data. A meta-language (a language to define languages) that has Hypertext Markup Language (HTML) capabilities. It is a language with many similarities to HTML and can be used to create HTML documents.
Extranet	A collaborative network that uses Internet technology to link businesses with their suppliers, customers, or other businesses that share common goals. An extranet can be viewed as part of a company's intranet that is made accessible to other companies or is used to collaborate with other companies. The shared information might be accessible only to the collaborating parties or, sometimes, the public.

F

Fiber Distributed Data Interface (FDDI)	It is an American National Standards Institute (ANSI) specification for fiber optics on local area networks that supports speeds of up to 100 megabits per second. It is a fiber optic interface that can extend a LAN's transmission range. It allows data to travel extreme distances (up to 200 km or 124 miles) without signal loss. The FDDI protocol is based on the token ring protocol and supports circuit-switched voice and data placed in packets.
Firewall	An application or an entire computer that controls access to a network and monitors the flow of network traffic. It is usually an Internet gateway server. It protects the resources of one network from users from other networks. Usually, an enterprise with an intranet that allows its workers access to the wider Internet will want a firewall to prevent outsiders from accessing its own private data

resources. The following is an example of a firewall architecture:

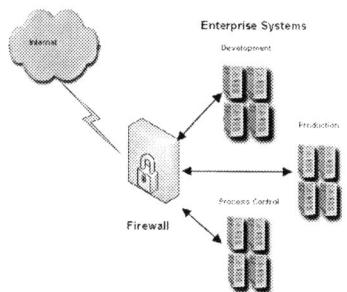

Figure 13. Example of firewall architecture.

Frequency-Division Multiplexing (FDM)

FDM is the division of a transmission frequency range into narrower bands to create two or more channels. It is a form of signal multiplexing in which multiple baseband signals are modulated on different frequency carrier waves and added together to create a composite signal. This enables each data source to have its own channel. In FDM, the multichannel transmission must originate from a single location. The following is a representative rudimentary diagram of how FDM works:

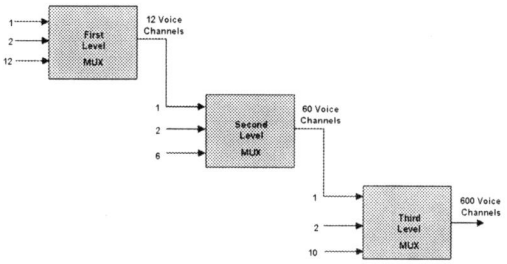

Figure 14. Example of frequency-division mutiplexing.

Function Points

Function points and the function point model are measurement tools to manage software. Function points, with other business measures, make up software metrics. Function points measure functionality by objectively measuring functional requirements. Function points are independent of the underlying system technology.

G

Gigabit

A billion bits. It is a unit of information or computer storage, abbreviated Gbit or sometimes Gb. It is exactly 2^{30}, or 1,073,741,824 bits.

Gigabyte

A billion bytes. It is a unit of information or computer storage equal to one billion bytes. It is commonly abbreviated GB in writing (not to be confused with Gb, which is used for gigabit). It is exactly 230, or 1,073,741,824 bytes.

Graphical User
Interface (GUI)

Any system that uses graphics to represent the functions of a computer program. It is a method of interacting with a computer through a metaphor of direct manipulation of graphical images and widgets in addition to text. It is sometimes pronounced *gooey*.

Graphics Interchange
Format (GIF)

It is a bitmap image format for pictures with up to 256 distinct colors or eight (8) bits. It is a standard that defines a mechanism for the storage and transmission of raster-based graphics information. It was invented by CompuServe for the efficient transmission of graphics.

H

Hypertext Markup
Language (HTML)

A standard language initially created for typesetting. It is a document-formatting language derived from SGML (see "Standard Generalized Markup Language"). It is mainly used for creating documents on the World Wide Web. One of the features of HTML is its ability to create hyperlinks that enable the user to navigate between documents. In addition, it has provisions for displaying graphics and links to other pages.

Hypertext Transfer Protocol (HTTP)	The underlying protocol used by the World Wide Web. It is the Internet standard for accessing and exchanging documents on the Web. A request /response, client/server protocol used to connect to Web servers.

I

Integrated Services Digital Network (ISDN)	An international communications standard that is a technical standard and design philosophy for digital networks. A type of circuit-switched telephone network system designed to allow digital transmission of voice, video, and data over ordinary telephone copper wires.
Interface Definition Language (IDL)	A computer language or syntax used to describe object interfaces by their names, methods, parameters, events, and return types. It is a computer language or simple syntax for describing the interface of a software component. A standard language for defining an object's abstract descriptions in their external interfaces.
International Organization for Standards (ISO)	A voluntary organization established in 1949 that is composed of representatives from national standards bodies. It is an organization that promotes the development of standards to aid in the international exchange of goods and services as well as develops mutual cooperation in areas of intellectual, scientific, technological, and economic activity.
Internet Message Access Protocol (IMAP)	A standard for retrieving Internet mail. It allows the user to create folders on the server. Those folders will show up in any e-mail client that is used. This protocol is used to access e-mail or bulletin board messages from a mail server. It allows a client e-mail

program to access remote message stores as if they were local. It is an application layer protocol.

Internet Protocol (IP)	The basic underlying protocol of the Internet. It is a data-oriented protocol used by both source and destination hosts for communicating data across a packet-switched network. It specifies the format of data packets (which are also called *datagram*) and the addressing method. Networks generally combine IP with the higher-level protocol, Transmission Control Protocol (TCP), which establishes a virtual connection between the source and destination hosts.
Internet Service Provider (ISP)	An enterprise that offers access to the Internet and related services. Generally, smaller ISPs buy bandwidth from larger ISPs. The ISP charges its customer a monthly fee. In return, the service provider gives the customer a software package, username, password, and access phone number that provides access to the Internet.
Internetwork Packet Exchange (IPX)	A networking protocol used by the Novell NetWare operating system. It is one of two gateway software techniques used to send and receive information between workstations and the network server. IPX allows concurrent dual access to both an application server and a native NetWare file server without using a lot of memory on the client workstation. The other technique is called NetBIOS.
ISDN Digital Subscriber Line (IDSL)	IDSL transmits data digitally on a regular twisted pair copper telephone line across existing ISDN lines. It provides dedicated service for digital data communications at speeds of up to 144 kilobits per second. The transfer rates for IDSL are about the same as ISDN (144kbps vs. 128kbps). However, IDSL circuits typically only carry data, not voice.

J

Joint Applications Development (JAD)	It is a process developed for designing computer-based systems. It brings together business area people (users) and IT professionals in a highly focused workshop session. It is an analytical fact-finding technique that allows users to be active participants in the development process. It has proven to be effective in the development of user interface requirements.
Joint Photographic Expert Group (JPEG)	A standard for photographic-image compression. It is designed for storing images with more than 256 colors in a small file size. It uses the *lossy* compression technique, which is a method of compressing data and then decompressing it to retrieve data that may be different from the original but is close enough to be useful. It provides the ability to set the amount of compression that is desired for the graphic.

K

Key Performance Indicator	A measurable quantity against which specific performance criteria can be set when drawing up a Service Level Agreement (SLA).
Key Success Indicator	A measurement of success or maturity of a project or process (see also "Critical Success Factor").
Kilobit	One thousand bits. Designated by either Kb or Kbit.
Kilobyte	One thousand bytes. Designated by either KB or Kbyte.
Kerberos	Kerberos is an authentication system developed at the Massachusetts Institute of Technology (MIT). It is used in networks to confirm that you are who you say you are. A person logs into a network and

an authentication server opens a session based on their password.

Knowledge Management

Discipline within an organization that ensures that the intellectual capabilities of an organization are shared, maintained, and institutionalized.

L

Latency

The elapsed time from the moment when a "seek" was completed on a disk device to the point when the required data is positioned under the read/write heads. It is normally defined by manufacturers as being half the disk rotation time.

Lightweight Directory Access Protocol (LDAP)

An industry-standard open client/server protocol for accessing a directory service, such as Active Directory or Novell Directory Services. It is a server-to-server interface for directory information exchange among directories.

Local Area Network (LAN)

A geographically limited communication network that connects users within a defined area. A LAN is generally contained within a building or small group of buildings and is managed and owned by a single enterprise. One LAN can be connected to other LANs over any distance via telephone lines and radio waves. A system of LANs connected in this way is called a wide-area network (see definition of *WAN*). Most LANs are likely to be based on switched Ethernet or Wi-Fi technology running at from 10 to 10,000 Mbps and do not have leased telephone lines.

Local Access and Transport Area (LATA)

A local telephone network area controlled and operated by a U.S. local-exchange carrier (LEC). A LATA represents a geographical area of the United States under the terms of the Modification of Final

Judgment (MFJ) entered by the United States District Court for the District of Columbia in Civil Action number 82-0192. In addition, it could be any other geographic area designated as a LATA in the National Exchange Carrier Association, Inc. Tariff FCC No. 4.

M

Mean Time Between Failures (MTBF)	The frequency of failures over a given time from the last resolution to the next incident.
Mean Time Between System Incidents (MTBSI)	A measure of the frequency of failure over a given time from one incident to the next.
Mean Time to Repair (MTTR)	The average time to restore a service or component to operability.
Messaging Application Program Interface (MAPI)	A standard programming interface from Microsoft that allows Windows applications to use the Windows e-mail system (such as Microsoft Exchange). It enables an application to send and receive mail over the e-mail messaging system.
Metropolitan Area Network (MAN)	Large computer networks that usually span a campus or a city. A collection of several LANs that are linked by a fast backbone connection. A MAN is smaller than a Wide Area Network (WAN) (e.g., college campus). MANs evolved from local area network (LAN) designs. They are optimized for longer distances (more than fifty kilometers) and greater speeds (more than a hundred megabits per second). In addition, they carry diverse forms of information (e.g., voice, data, image, and video).
Moving Picture Experts Group (MPEG)	The family of digital video compression standards and file formats developed by the working group of ISO/IEC. The compression ratios of MPEG encoding make it an effective standard for the

delivery of digital video data. The MPEG formats are the following:

- MPEG-1: A group of audio and video coding standards used by the video CD format and includes the popular Layer 3 (MP3) audio compression format.
- MPEG-2: Transport, video, and audio standards for broadcast-quality television. It is typically used to encode audio and video for broadcast signals, including direct broadcast satellite and cable TV.
- MPEG-3: Originally designed for HDTV but abandoned when it was discovered that MPEG-2 was sufficient for HDTV.
- MPEG-4: It is a graphics and video compression algorithm standard that is based on MPEG-1 and MPEG-2. Originally introduced in 1988, it is primarily used for the World Wide Web (streaming media), CD distribution, and conversational (videophone) and broadcast television.
- MPEG-7: A formal system for describing multimedia content.

Multipurpose Internet Mail Extension (MIME)	An Internet standard for the format of e-mail. It is a set of functions that enables the transport of attachments and nonstandard text via Simple Message Transport Protocol (SMTP).

N

Nanosecond	One billionth of a second. It is generally used to measure the speed of computer memory. One nanosecond equals 10^{-9} seconds.

Nanotechnology	The focused treatment of matter at the atomic level to achieve a distinct goal. Nanotechnology generally refers to technological developments on the nanometer scale. One nanometer equals one thousandth of a micrometer.
Network Basic Input/Output System (NetBIOS)	One of two gateway software techniques used to send and receive information between workstations and the network server. NetBIOS allows applications on separate computers to communicate over a local area network. It provides services related to the session layer (see "OSI Reference Model").
Network File System (NFS)	A method of sharing files across a computer network. It is a protocol that was originally developed by Sun Microsystems in 1984. It is a client/server application that allows all network users to access shared files stored on computers of different types.
Network News Transport Protocol (NNTP)	It is an Internet application protocol that is used to transfer news among news servers. A database standard that governs USENET newsgroup distribution on the Internet. It is used to post, distribute, and retrieve USENET messages.

O

Object Linking & Embedding (OLE)	A distributed object system and protocol. It was developed by Microsoft to enable the creation of compound documents with embedded links to applications. This is done so that a user does not have to switch from one application to another to make revisions.
Object Request Broker (ORB)	A component in the CORBA programming model that acts as the middleware between clients and servers. It allows objects to communicate with other software.

Online Analytical
Processing (OLAP)

A category of business intelligence tools used to analyze data. The objective is to quickly provide the answer to complex analytical queries. It is a group of technologies and applications that collect, manage, process, and present data for analysis and management purposes. OLAP tools enable users to analyze different dimensions of multidimensional data.

Online Transaction
Processing (OLTP)

A form of transaction processing conducted via computer network. It is a mode of processing that is distinguished by short transactions recording business events. It normally requires high availability and consistent, short response times. It allows real-time inputting, recording, and retrieval of data to/from a networked system.

Open Database
Connectivity (ODBC)

A standard software application program interface (API) specification for using database management systems (DBMS). It is a vendor-neutral interface based on the Structured Query Language (SQL) specifications. It is designed to be independent of the programming language, database system, and operating system.

Open Source

The source code of a program that is freely accessible to the entire software development community. This source code is generally accessed though the Internet. The underlying principle behind the *freely shared* idea is that a broader group of programmers will ultimately produce a better product. Developers from around the world could distribute their code to other programmers anywhere in the world. UNIX and Linux are the most popular open source codes.

Open Systems Inter-
connection (OSI) Reference
Model

A standard to allow various *open* systems to communicate with one another. Developed by the International Organization for Standardization (ISO), the OSI reference model establishes guidelines for network architectures. The OSI reference model divides the network communications functions into seven layers. The following depicts the seven layers and their function:

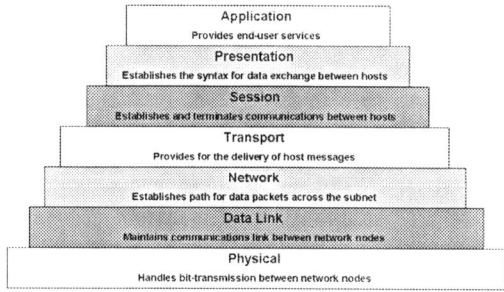

Figure 15. Open Systems Interconnection (OSI) reference model.

| Operational Costs | The costs resulting from the day-to-day running of IT services (e.g., staff costs, hardware maintenance, and electricity) and relating to repeating payments whose effects can be measured within a short time-frame, usually less than the twelve-month financial year. |

| Operational Level Agreement (OLA) | An internal agreement covering the delivery of services that support the IT organization in their delivery of services (also see "Service Level Agreements"). |

| Opportunity Cost (or true cost) | The value of a benefit sacrificed in favor of an alternative course of action. That is the cost of using resources in a particular operation expressed in forgoing the benefit that could be derived from the best alternative use of those resources. |

P

| Package Assembly / Disassembly Device (PAD) | A device that permits terminals, which do not have an interface suitable for direct connection to a packet switched network, to access such a network. A |

PAD converts data to/from packets and handles call set-up and addressing.

Page Fault

A program interruption that occurs within the computer when a page that is marked "not in real memory" is referred to by an active page.

Paging

The input/output necessary to read and write to and from the paging disks; real (not virtual) memory is needed to process data. With insufficient real memory, the operating system writes old pages to disk and reads new pages from disk, so that the required data and instructions are in real memory when needed.

Percentage Utilization

The amount of time that a hardware device is busy over a given period of time. For example, if the CPU is busy for 1800 seconds in a one-hour period, its utilization is said to be 50 percent.

Performance Criteria

The expected levels of achievement which are set within the service level agreement (SLA) against specific key performance indicators (KPI).

Petabyte

A petabyte is 250 bytes. This is approximately one thousand terabytes, one million gigabytes, one billion megabytes, one trillion kilobytes, or one quadrillion bytes.

Physical I/O

A read or write request from a program that has necessitated a physical read or write operation on an input/output device.

Point of Presence (POP)

It is usually the point at which the local telephone company terminates subscribers' circuits for access to long-distance service. It is a physical location that is either part of the facilities of a telecommunications provider that the Internet service provider (ISP) rents or a separate location from the telecommunications provider. If it is the site of the telecommunications provider, it will be where the servers, routers, ATM switches, and digital/analog call aggregators are located.

Portable Operating System Interface-UNIX (POSIX)	A set of operating system interface standards based on UNIX that defines the application programming interface (API) for software compatible with variants of the UNIX operating system. Developers that design their programs to conform to POSIX, have some assurance that their software can be easily ported to POSIX-compliant operating systems.
Post Office Protocol (POP)	A protocol that provides a mailbox-retrieval service for Internet users. It is an application-layer Internet standard protocol for the retrieval of e-mail from a remote server over a TCP/IP connection. There are two versions of POP. The first, called POP2, was a standard in the mid 1980s and required the Simple Mail Transfer Protocol (SMTP) to send messages. The more recent version is POP3, which can be used with or without SMTP.
Pretty Good Privacy (PGP)	Security applications for Internet e-mail that uses a variety of encryption standards and is freely available for all major operating systems.
Prime Cost	The total cost of direct materials, direct labor, and direct expenses. The term *prime cost* is commonly restricted to direct production costs only and so does not customarily include direct costs of marketing or research and development.
PRINCE2	The standard UK government method for project management.
Problem Management	Process that minimizes the effect on customers of defects in services and within the infrastructure, human errors, and external events.

Program Information File (PIF)	A file type that holds information about how Windows should run a non-Windows application. It defines how a given Windows program should be run in a multitasking environment.
Public Key Cryptography	It is a cryptography technique that combines the use of a private and public key. The recipient has both a private and public key, and senders use the public key to send a message. The recipient uses the tightly held private key to decode the message. Since the recipient is the only one with the private key and since the key is never sent over the Internet, the message is more secure.
	The most popular scheme is called RSA (named for its inventors, Ronald Rivest, Adi Shamir, and Leonard Adleman). It is an Internet encryption and authentication standard that uses a complex mathematical algorithm to determine two numbers. These numbers are also called *keys*. One is set up as the private key and the other is made public. The private key decodes text that has been coded with the public key. The RSA algorithm is incorporated into the Microsoft and Netscape Web browsers.

Q

Quality of Service (QoS)	An agreed-upon or contracted level of service between a service customer and a service provider.
Queuing Time	Queuing time is incurred when the device, which a program wishes to use, is already busy. The program has to wait in a queue to obtain service from that device.

R

Redundant Array of Inexpensive Disks (RAID)	A mechanism for providing data resilience for computer systems using mirrored arrays of magnetic disks. Different levels of RAID can be applied to provide for greater resilience.
Release	A collection of new and/or modified change items (CI) that are tested and introduced into the live environment together.
Request For Change (RFC)	Form or screen used to record details of a request for a change to any change tem (CI) within an infrastructure, or to procedures and items associated with the infrastructure.
Return On Investment (ROI)	The ratio of the cost of implementing a project, product, or service and the savings as a result of completing the activity. It is stated in internal savings, increased external revenue, or a combination of the two. For instance, if the internal cost of cabling office moves is $100,000 per year and a structured cabling system can be installed for $300,000, then an ROI will be achieved after approximately three years.
Rich Text Format (RTF)	A document file format that is used for cross-platform document interchange. They are ASCII files with particular commands to indicate formatting of information such as fonts, margins, and boldness.
Risk	A measure of the harmful exposure to which an organization may be subjected. This is a combination of the likelihood of a business disruption occurring and the possible loss that may result from such business disruption.
Risk Analysis	The process for determining the value of the assets at risk. The identification and assessment of the

level (measure) of the risk calculated from the assessed values of assets and the assessed levels of threats to, and vulnerabilities of, those assets.

Risk Management
The identification, selection, and adoption of countermeasures justified by the identified risks to assets in their potential impact upon services if a failure occurs, and the reduction of those risks to an acceptable level.

Risk Reduction Measure
Measures taken to reduce the likelihood or consequences of a business disruption occurring (as opposed to planning to recover after a disruption).

Rotational Position Sensing
A facility employed on most mainframes and some minicomputers. When a *seek* has been initiated, the system can free the path from a disk drive to a controller for use by another disk drive while it is waiting for the required data to come under the read/write heads (latency). This facility usually improves the overall performance of the input/output subsystem.

S

SCRUM
An agile method for project development. It is a development approach that is designed as an enhancement of the iterative and incremental approach to delivering object-oriented software.

Secure Sockets Layer (SSL)
A cryptographic protocol used for transmitting private documents via the Internet. It uses public key encryption, including digital certificates and digital signatures, to pass data between a browser and a server. SSL has recently been succeeded by Transport Layer Security (TLS), which is based on SSL. The SSL program layer is located between the Internet's Hypertext Transfer Protocol (HTTP) and Transport Control Protocol (TCP) layers.

Security Management	The process of managing a defined level of security on information and services.
Seek Time	Occurs when the disk read/write heads are not positioned on the required track. It describes the elapsed time taken to move heads to the correct track.
Service Level Agreement (SLA)	An agreement that sets the expectations between a service provider and its customer. For an ISP, it is a promise to maintain a consistent level of data transfer over a network. An SLA describes the products or services to be delivered; the availability of data and the network, and the point of contact for end-user problems. In addition, it outlines how the services will be measured and managed.
Service Level Management (SLM)	The process of defining, agreeing, documenting, and managing the levels of customer IT service that is required and cost-justified.
Service Quality Plan	The written plan and specification of internal targets designed to guarantee the agreed service levels.
Severity Code	Simple code assigned to problems and known errors, indicating the seriousness of their effect on the quality of service (QoS). It is the major means of assigning priority for resolution.
Simple Mail Transfer Protocol (SMTP)	The Internet standard for transferring e-mail. It is a server-to-server protocol that supports only text. This protocol cannot handle e-mail attachments. E-mail attachments can be sent using the Multipurpose Internet Mail Extension (MIME) standard.
Simple Network Management Protocol (SNMP)	A set of protocols for managing complex netw works. It is a Transmission Control Protocol/Internet Protocol (TCP/IP), which governs network management and the monitoring of network devices. It

is used to manage network devices such as hubs and routers.

Simple Object Access Protocol (SOAP)

It is a lightweight protocol for exchange of information in a decentralized, distributed environment. The protocol is entirely based upon XML, is vendor-neutral, and is one of the cornerstone technologies in Web services. It represents the invocation mechanism within a Web service architecture.

Simulation Modeling

Using a program to simulate computer processing by describing in detail the path of a job or transaction. It can give extremely accurate results. Unfortunately, it demands a great deal of time and effort from the modeler. It is most beneficial in extremely large or time-critical systems where the margin for error is very small.

Small Computer Systems Interface (SCSI)

Pronounced *skuzzy*, it is the fastest and generally, most flexible method of interfacing with hard drives. SCSI provides a high-speed, parallel data transfer of up to 40 Mbps. It has the advantage of connecting multiple peripherals while taking up only one slot in the computer. It is a standard data pathway used for hard drives, CD-ROM drives, scanners, and printers.

Soft Fault

The situation in a virtual memory system when the operating system has detected that a page of code or data was due to be reused (i.e., it is on a list of free pages), but it is still in memory. It is now recovered and put back into service.

Solid State Devices

Memory devices that are made to appear as if they are disk devices. The advantage of such devices is that the service times are much faster than real disks since there is no seek time or latency. The main disadvantage is that they are much more expensive.

Standard Cost	A predetermined calculation of how many costs should be incurred under specified working conditions. It is built from an assessment of the value of cost elements and correlates technical specifications and the quantification of materials, labor, and other costs to the prices and/or wages expected to apply during the period in which the standard cost is intended to be used. Its main purposes are to provide basis for control through variance accounting, for the valuation of work in progress, and for fixing selling prices.
Standard Costing	A technique that uses standards for costs and revenues to control through variance analysis.
Standard Generalized Markup Language (SGML)	A system for organizing and tagging elements of a document. It is a standard for the markup of electronic documents developed in 1986 by the International Organization for Standardization (ISO). SGML itself does not specify any particular formatting. It does specify the rules for tagging the elements of a document.
Stand-By Arrangements	Arrangements to have available assets that have been identified as replacements should primary assets be unavailable following a business disruption. Typically, these include buildings, IT systems and networks, telecommunications, and sometimes people.
Storage Area Network (SAN)	A high-speed sub-network of shared storage devices. It is a storage system consisting of storage elements, storage devices, computer systems, and/or appliances, plus all of the necessary control software communicating over a network. It provides the ability to transfer data between computer systems and storage elements as well as between the different storage elements.

Strategic Alignment
Objectives Model (SAOM)

A diagram depicting the relation between a business function and its business drivers, and the technology with the technology characteristics. The SAOM is a high-level tool that can help IT services organizations align their service level agreements, operational level agreements, and acceptance criteria for new technology with the business value they deliver.

Swapping

The reaction of the operating system to insufficient real memory. Swapping occurs when too many tasks are perceived to be competing for limited resources. It is the physical movement of an entire task. For example, all real memory pages of an address space may be moved at one time from main storage to auxiliary storage.

Symmetric
Multiprocessing (SMP)

A multiprocessor computer architecture where two or more identical processors are connected to a single shared main memory. The processors execute both user and operating-system code. It provides a high level of performance by making multiple CPUs available to complete individual processes simultaneously.

T

Terabit

One trillion bits. Designated as either Tb or Tbit.

Terabyte

One trillion bytes. Designated as either TB or Tbyte.

Thrashing

A condition in a virtual storage system where an excessive proportion of CPU time is spent moving data between main and auxiliary storage.

Threat

An indication of an unwanted incident that could impinge on the system in some way. Threats may be deliberate (e.g., willful damage) or accidental (e.g., operator or inadvertent error).

Time Division Multiplexing (TDM)

A data, voice, and video communications technique that multiplexes several low-speed signals into one high-speed transmission channel by allocating brief, interleaved time periods to each signal. Sharing of the signal is accomplished by dividing available transmission time on a medium among users. Digital signaling is used exclusively. Time division multiplexing comes in two basic forms:

1   Synchronous: The multiplexer accepts input from attached devices in a *round-robin* fashion and transmits the data in a never-ending pattern.

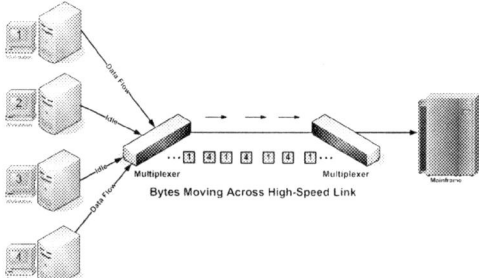

Figure 16. Synchronous time division multiplexing.

2   Statistical or asynchronous: A statistical multiplexer transmits only the data from active workstations.

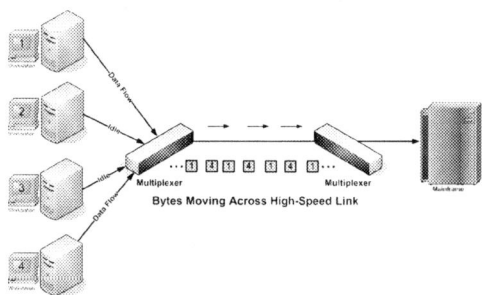

Figure 17. Statistical time division multiplexing.

Total Cost of Ownership (TCO)	A calculation that considers all costs associated with investment in a technology. It is calculated by including depreciation, maintenance, staff costs, accommodation, and planned renewal.
Transport Control Protocol (TCP)	A protocol that handles reliable delivery of messages of arbitrary size, and defines a robust delivery mechanism for all kinds of data across a network. It is a communications protocol based on the U.S. Department of Defense's standards for reliable internetwork delivery of data.
Transport Layer Security (TLS)	A protocol that ensures privacy between communicating applications and their users on the Internet. It is a protocol sponsored by the Internet Engineering Task Force (IETF) and is intended to secure and authenticate communications across a public network through data encryption. It allows applications to communicate in a client/server environment in a way that prevents eavesdropping, tampering, or message forgery.

U

Universal Description, Discover, and Integration (UDDI)	A platform-independent, XML-based registry for businesses worldwide to list themselves on the Internet. It specifies a standard format with which enterprises can describe themselves and their method of conducting e-business transactions, within an Internet-based business registry. Businesses can discover each other similar to a traditional phone book's yellow and white pages.
Unabsorbed Overhead	Any indirect cost that cannot be apportioned to a specific customer.

V

Variance Analysis	A variance is the difference between planned, budgeted, or standard cost, and actual cost (or revenues). Variance analysis is an analysis of the factors

that have caused the difference between the predetermined standards and the actual results. Variances can be developed specifically related to the operations carried out, in addition to those mentioned above.

Vendor Management Office A vendor management office (VMO) is set up in the IT department of a company to manage multiple vendor relationships. They will generally handle all of the complicated negotiations with the major IT vendors. In addition, the VMO manages the request for information (RFI) and request for proposal (RFP) processes, works with legal on all contract work, manages the ongoing operational and financial aspects of the contract, establishes internal vendor policies and procedures, and maintains the relationships with all vendors.

Version An identified instance of a configuration item within a product breakdown structure or configuration structure for tracking and auditing change history. Also used for software configuration items to define a specific identification released in development for drafting, review or modification, test or production.

Very Large Scale Integration (VLSI) The amount of transistors incorporated in a chip. An integrated circuit (IC) consisting of 10,000 to 99,999 logic gates. The technology makes it possible to place the equivalent of between 100,000 and 1 million transistors on a chip.

Video Graphics Array (VGA) A hardware display and software resolution standard for personal computers. It was developed by IBM and introduced in 1987. VGA provides 640 × 480 resolution color display screens with a refresh rate of 60Hz and 16 colors displayed at a time.

Virtual Memory System (VMS)	A system that enhances the size of hard memory by adding an auxiliary storage layer residing on the hard disk.
Virtual Private Network (VPN)	A private network that uses a public network (usually the Internet) to connect remote sites or users together. Instead of using a dedicated connection such as a leased line, a VPN uses "virtual" connections routed though the Internet. It provides customized operating characteristics uniformly and universally across an enterprise. It uses encryption software or hardware to bring privacy to the enterprise communications.
Voice Over Internet Protocol (VoIP)	VoIP is the transmission of voice communications over Internet Protocol (IP) data networks, such as LANs, intranets, or the Internet. It is sometimes referred to as IP telephony or Internet telephony. The voice data flows over a general purpose packet-switched network, instead of traditional dedicated, circuit-switched voice transmission lines. The following is a system model for VoIP:

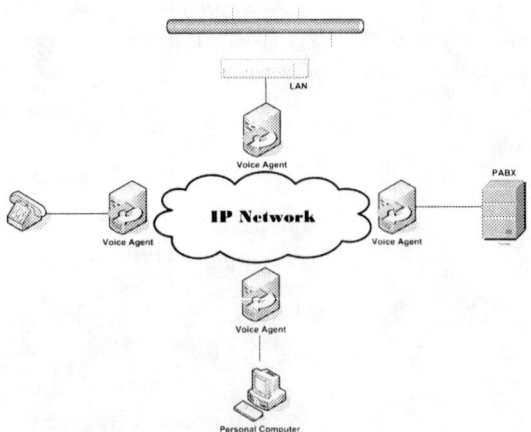

Figure 18. System model of Voice over IP (VoIP).

Vulnerability	A weakness of the system and its assets, which could be exploited by threats.

W

Wide Area Network (WAN)	A communications network that connects computing devices over a wide, geographically dispersed area involving an immense array of computers. Computers connected to a wide-area network can be connected through public networks, leased lines, or satellites. A WAN covers a much larger area than a LAN (local area network) or MAN (metropolitan area network). A WAN could cover a city, state, or country. An example of and extremely large WAN is the Internet.
Web Services	Web services provide a standard means of interoperating between different software applications, running on a variety of platforms and/or frameworks. Web services, as a concept, treats software as a set of services accessible over omnipresent networks using Web-based standards and protocols. It is both a software concept and an infrastructure that is supported by several major computing vendors. It is primarily used for program-to-program communication and application component delivery.
Work-around	Method of avoiding an incident or problem, either from a temporary fix or from a technique that means the customer is not reliant on a particular aspect of the service that is known to have a problem.
Workloads	In the context of Capacity Management Modeling, a set of forecasts that detail the estimated resource usage over an agreed planning horizon. Workloads generally represent discrete business applications and can be further subdivided into types of work (interactive, timesharing, batch).

| WORM (Device) | Optical read only disks, standing for Write Once Read Many. |

X

| XML (eXtensible Markup Language) | XML is a set of rules for designing text formats that let you structure your data (see "Extensible Markup Language"). XML makes it easy for a computer to generate data, read data, and ensure that the data structure is unambiguous. XML avoids common pitfalls in language design. It is extensible, platform-independent, and it supports internationalization as well as localization. |

Z

| Zero Latency | The removal of delays in the movement of information, data, or goods. |
| Zip | A popular data compression and archival format. A ZIP file contains one or more files that have been compressed or stored in to one file. These compressed files will contain the file extension, "zip." |

Acronyms & Abbreviations

It used to always drive me crazy when people used acronyms and just expected everyone in the room to know what they were talking about. I guarantee you that your technical wizards will do it to you over and over again. Well, before you stress out over the situation, come to this section and look it up.

A number next to the acronym means that this is the second or third definition for this acronym. That's right, there could be more than one definition for the same set of letters. (Great, right?) Therefore, when looking up the acronym, make sure you understand the context in which it was used to ensure that you are retrieving the correct one. If you heard an acronym that is not in the list, drop me an email at wayne@apsg-ltd.com, and I will e-mail you with a definition (assuming one exists) and incorporate it into future editions of this book.

I hope this helps.

A

AA	Administrative Authority
AAL	ATM Adaption Layer
AARP	AppleTalk Address Resolution Protocol
ABM	Asynchronous Balanced Mode
ACD	Automatic Call Director
ACH	Automated Clearing House
ACK	Acknowledgment
ACS	Asynchronous Communication Server
ADO	ActiveX Data Objects
ADSL	Asymmetric Digital Subscriber Line
ADSP	AppleTalk Data Stream Protocol
AEP	AppleTalk Echo Protocol
AFRP	ARCNET Fragmentation Protocol
AFS	Andrew File System
AGP	Accelerated Graphics Port
AGS	Asynchronous Gateway Server
AI	Artificial Intelligence
AIN	Advanced Intelligent Network
AIX	Advanced Interactive eXecutive

ALU	Arithmetic Logic Unit
AM	Amplitude Modulation
AMD	Advanced Micro Devices
AMDB	Availability Management Database
AMPS	Advanced Mobile Phone Service
AMS	Application Management Specification
ANSI	American National Standards Institute
API	Application Program Interface
APPC	Advanced Program-to-Program Communications
APPN	Advanced Peer-to-Peer Networking
ARM	Asynchronous Response Mode
ARP	Address Resolution Protocol
ARPA	Advanced Research Projects Agency
ARPANET	Advanced Research Projects Agency Network
ASCII	American Standard Code for Information Interchange
ASM	Association for Systems Management
ASP	Application Service Provider
ASP (2)	AppleTalk Session Protocol
ASP (3)	Active Server Pages
ATM	Asynchronous Transfer Mode
ATP	AppleTalk Transaction Protocol

B

BASIC	Beginners All-Purpose Symbolic Instruction Code
BCD	Binary Coded Decimal
BGP	Border Gateway Protocol
BIOS	Basic Input/Output System
BISDN	Broadband Integrated Services Digital Network
BPI	Business Process Improvement
BPM	Business Process Modeling
BPML	Business Process Modeling Language
BPO	Business Process Outsourcers
BPR	Business Process Reengineering
BOC	Bell Operating Company
BOM	Beginning of Message
Bps	Bits Per Second
BSA	Business Software Alliance
BSC	Bisynchronous Communications
BSS	Broadband Switching System
BTU	Basic Transmission Unit

C

CA	Certificate Authority
CAD	Computer-Aided Design
CAM	Computer-Aided Manufacturing
CAM (2)	Channel Access Method
CAM (3)	Common Access Method
CASE	Computer Aided Software Engineering
CBD	Component-Based Development
CBT	Computer-Based Training
CCIE	Cisco Certified Internetwork Expert
CCIE-R&S	Cisco Certified Internetwork Expert-Routing & Switching
CCIE-S	Cisco Certified Internetwork Expert-Security
CCIE-SP	Cisco Certified Internetwork Expert-Service Provider
CCIE-V	Cisco Certified Internetwork Expert-Voice
CCITT	Consultative Committee for International Telephone & Telegraph
CCNA	Cisco Certified Network Associate
CCNP	Cisco Certified Network Professional
CDDI	Copper Distributed Data Interface
CDE	Common Development Environment
CDMA	Code Division Multiple Access
CDPD	Cellular Digital Packet Data
CDSA	Common Data Security Architecture
CEO	Chief Executive Officer
CFO	Chief Financial Officer
CFI	Common Intermediate Format
CGA	Color Graphics Adapter
CGI	Common Gateway Interface
CGI (2)	Computer Generated Imagery
CI	Configuration Item
CICS	Customer Information & Control System
CIO	Chief Information Officer
CIP	Certified Internet Professional
CLP	Certified Lotus Professional
CMM	Capability Maturity Model
CMO	Chief Marketing Officer
CNA	Certified Novell Administrator
CNE	Certified Novell Engineer
CNI	Certified Novell Instructor

CNS	Certified Novell Salesperson
CO	Central Office
COBIT	Control Objectives for Information and related Technology
COBOL	Common Business Oriented Language
COE	Centers of Excellence
COM	Component Object Module
COTS	Commercial Off-the-Shelf Software
CORBA	Common Object Request Broker Architecture
COSE	Common Open Software Environment
CPE	Customer Premise Equipment
CP/M	Control Program/Microcomputer
CPS	Characters Per Second
CPU	Central Processing Unit
CRC	Cyclical Redundancy Check
CRT	Cathode Ray Tube
CSIRT	Computer Security Incident Response Teams
CSLIP	Compressed Serial Line Internet Protocol
CSP	Certified Systems Professional
CSPDN	Circuit Switched Public Data Network
CTO	Chief Technology Officer
CUA	Common User Access
CWO	Chief Web Officer

D

DAMPS	Digital Advanced Mobile Phone Service
DARPA	Defense Advanced Research Projects Agency
DBMS	Database Management System
DCA	Defense Communications Agency
DCE	Distributed Computing Environment
DCE (2)	Data Circuit-Terminating Equipment
DCE (3)	Data Communication Equipment
DCN	Data Communications Network
DCOM	Distributed Component Object Module
DDE	Dynamic Data Exchange
DDL	Data Definition Language
DDN	Defense Data Network
DDP	Datagram Delivery Protocol
DDS	Digital Data Service
DES	Data Encryption Standard

DFS	Distributed File System
DHCP	Dynamic Host Configuration Protocol
DHTML	Dynamic HTML
DID	Direct Inward Dialing
DLC	Data Link Control
DLL	Dynamic Link Library
DMA	Direct Memory Access
DME	Distributed Management Environment
DMZ	Demilitarized Zone
DNA	Digital Network Architecture
DNS	Domain Naming Service
DOE	Distributed Objects Everywhere
DOM	Document Access Model
DOS	Disk Operating System
Dpi	Dots per Inch
DPMA	Data Processing Management Association
DRDA	Distributed Relational Database Architecture
DRP	Distributed Request Protocol
DS0	Digital Signal Level 0 (64 kbps)
DS1	Digital Signal Level 1 (1.544 Mbps)
DS3	Digital Signal Level 3 (44.736 Mbps)
DSA	Digital Signature Algorithm (same as DSS)
DSDM	Dynamic Systems Development Method
DSL	Digital Subscriber Line
DSML	Directory Services Markup Language
DSOM	Distributed System Object Module
DSP	Directory System Protocol
DSS	Digital Signature Standard (same as DSA)
DSU	Data Service Unit
DTE	Data Terminal Equipment
DVD	Digital Versatile Disk

E

EBCDIC	Extended Binary Coded Decimal Interchange Code
ebXML	Electronic Business XML
EDI	Electronic Data Interchange
EDFACT	Electronic Data Interchange for Administration, Commerce & Transportation

EFT	Electronic Funds Transfer
EGA	Enhanced Graphics Array
EGP	Exterior Gateway Protocol

E-MAIL Acronyms	AFK:	Away from keyboard
	BAK:	Back at keyboard
	BRB:	Be right back
	BTW:	By the way
	FWIW:	For what it's worth
	GMTA:	Great minds think alike
	IAC:	In any case
	IMHO:	In my humble opinion
	IMNSHO:	In my not-so-humble opinion
	LOL:	Laughing out loud
	ROFL:	Rolling on floor laughing
	TTFN:	Ta ta for now
	TTYL:	Talk to you later
	YMMV:	Your mileage may vary
	WB:	Welcome back
	WTG:	Way to go

EMM	Extended Memory Manager
EPROM	Erasable Programmable Read Only Memory
ERP	Enterprise Resource Planning
ETSI	European Telecommunications Standards Institute
EULA	End User License Agreement

F

FAT	File Access Table
FCC	Federal Communications Commission
FDDI	Fiber Distributed Data Interface
FDM	Frequency Division Multiplexing
FDMA	Frequency Division Multiple Access
FEP	Front End Processor
FIPS	Federal Information Processing Standard
FM	Frequency Modulation
FORTRAN	Formula Translator
FOTS	Fiber Optics Transport System
FR	Frame Relay
FT1	Fractional T1

FTAM	File Transfer Access and Management
FTP	File Transfer Protocol

G

G	Giga
Gbps	Gigabits Per Second
GB	Gigabyte
GBps	Gigabytes Per Second
GDI	Graphics Device Interface
GDS	Global Directory Service
GHz	Gigahertz
GIF	Graphics Interchange Format
GIGO	Garbage In Garbage Out
GOSIP	Government Open Systems Interconnect Profile
GPI	Graphical Programming Interface
GSM	Global System for Mobile Communications
GUI	Graphical User Interface

H

HCI	Human Computer Interface
HDLC	High Level Data Link Control
HDML	Handheld Device Markup Language
HDSL	High-bit-rate Digital Subscriber Line
HDSL (2)	High-level Data Specification Language
HFS	Hierarchical File System
HLLAPI	High Level Language Application Program Interface
HPFS	High Performance File System
HTML	Hypertext Markup Language
HTTP	Hypertext Transfer Protocol
HWG	HTML Writers Guild
Hz	Hertz

I

IBM CATE	BM Certified Advanced Technical Expert
IBM CD	IBM Certified Developer
IBM CDA	IBM Certified Developer Associate
IBM CI	IBM Certified Instructor
IBM CS	IBM Certified Specialist

IBM CSE	IBM Certified Solutions/Systems Expert
ICE	Information Content Exchange Protocol
ICMP	Internet Control Message Protocol
ICP	Internet Control Protocol
IDEA	International Data Encryption Algorithm
IDL	nterface Definition Language
IDP	Internetwork Datagram Protocol
IDSL	ISDN Digital Subscriber Line
IDU	Interface Data Unit
IEC	International Electrotechnical Commission
IEEE	Institute of Electrical and Electronics Engineers
IGP	Interior Gateway Protocol
IGRP	Internet Gateway Routing Protocol
IMS	Information Management System
ILM	Information Life cycle Management
IMAP	Internet Message Access Protocol
IP	Internet Protocol
IPC	Interprocess Communication Protocol
IPL	Initial Program Load
IPX	Internetwork Packet Exchange
ISA	Industry Standard Architecture
ISAPI	Internet Server Application Programmer's Interface
ISDN	Integrated Services Digital Network
ISO	International Standards Organization
ISP	Internet Service Provider
ISP (2)	Integrated System Peripheral control
ISP (3)	Integrated Support Plan
ITAA	Information Technology Association of America
ITSP	Internet Telephony Service Provider
ITU	International Telecommunication Union

J

JAD	Joint Applications Development
JECF	Java Electronic Commerce Framework
JEPI	Joint Electronic Payments Initiative
JPEG	Joint Photographic Experts Group
JTAPI	Java Telephony API
JVM	Java Virtual Machine

K

Kbps	Kilobits Per Second
KB	Kilobyte
KHz	Kilohertz

L

LAN	Local Area Network
LAP	Link Access Protocol
LAT	Local Area Transport
LATA	Local Area Transport Area
LCD	Liquid Crystal Display
LDAP	Lightweight Directory Access Protocol
LE	Local Exchange
LEC	Local Exchange Carrier
LED	Light Emitting Diode
LFS	Local File System
LLC	Logical Link Control
LSA	Local Security Authority
LU	Logical Unit
LUN	Logical Unit Number

M

MAC	Media Access Control
MAN	Metropolitan Area Network
MAP	Management Application Protocol
MAP (2)	Manufacturing Automation Protocol
MAPI	Messaging Application Program Interface
MAU	Multiple Access Unit
Mbps	Mega Bits Per Second
MB	Megabyte
MCA	Micro Channel Architecture
MCBA	Microsoft Certified Database Administrator
MCGA	Multicolor Graphics Array
MCP	Microsoft Certified Professional
MCSD	Microsoft Certified Solution Developer
MCSE	Microsoft Certified Systems Engineer

MCT	Microsoft Certified Trainer
MCU	Multipoint Control Unit
MDBS	Mobile Database Station
MHz	Megahertz
MIDI	Musical Instrument Digital Interface
MIME	Multimedia Internet Mail Extension
MIPS	Millions Instructions Per Second
MODEM	Modulator / Demodulator
MOM	Message Oriented Middleware
MOS	Metal Oxide Semiconductor
MPEG	Moving Picture Experts Group
MPLS	Multi-Protocol Label Switching ms Milliseconds
MSAU	Multi Station Access Unit
MTA	Message Transfer Agent
MTBF	Mean Time Between Failures
MTBSI	Mean Time Between System Incidents
MTTR	Mean Time To Repair
MUX	Multiplexer
MVS	Multiple Virtual Storage

N

NAK	Negative Acknowledgment
NAP	Network Access Points
NAS	Network Attached Storage
NAT	Network Address Translation
NC	Network Computer
NCP	Network Control Program
NCP (2)	Network Core Protocols
NetBIOS	Network Basic Input / Output System
NFS	Network File System
NIC	Network Information Center
NIC (2)	Network Interface Card
NIC (3)	Network Independent Clock
NIST	National Institute of Standards and Technology
NMS	Network Management System
NNTP	Network News Transport Protocol
NOC	Network Operations Center
NOS	Network Operating System
NSF	National Science Foundation
NSP	Network Services Protocol

| NT | New Technology |
| NTFS | Windows NT File System |

O

OC1	Optical Carrier, Level 1 (51.84 Mbps)
OC3	Optical Carrier, Level 3 (155.52 Mbps)
Ocn	Optical Carrier, Level n
OCR	Optical Character Recognition
ODBC	Open Database Connectivity
ODI	Open Data Link Interface
OEM	Original Equipment Manufacturer
OID	Object Identifier
OLAP	Online Analytical Processing
OLE	Object Linking and Embedding
OLTP	On-Line Transaction Processing
OMA	Object Management Architecture
OMG	Object Management Group
OML	Object Manipulation Language
ONC	Open Network Computing
OOA	Object-Oriented Analysis
OOD	Object-Oriented Design
OOP	Object-Oriented Programming
OOUI	Object-Oriented User Interface
ORB	Object Request Broker
OS	Operating System
OSF	Open Software Foundation
OSI	Open Systems Interconnection
OSI-RM	Open Systems Interconnection Reference Model

P

P3P	Platform for Privacy Preferences Project (W3C)
P&S	Publish & Subscribe
PABX	Private Automatic Branch Exchange
PAP	Password Authentication Protocol
PARC	Palo Alto Research Center
PB	Petabyte
PBX	Private Branch Exchange
PCI	Protocol Control Information

PCI (2)	Peripheral Component Interconnect
PCM	Pulse Code Modulation
PCMCIA	Personal Computer Memory Card Interface Architecture
PDA	Personal Digital Assistants
PDC	Primary Domain Controller
PDF	Portable Document Format
PDF (2)	Program Development Facility
PDF (3)	Postscript Document Format
PDN	Public Data Network
PDU	Protocol Data Unit
PEM	Privacy Enhanced Mail
PEP	Packet Exchange Protocol
PERL	Practical Extraction and Report Language
PGA	Pin Grid Array
PGP	Pretty Good Privacy
PICS	Platform for Internet Content Selection
PID	Protocol Identifier
PIF	Program Information File
PKI	Public Key Infrastructure
PLP	Packet Layer Protocol
PNP	Plug and Play
POP	Point of Presence
POP (2)	Post Office Protocol
POSIX	Portable Operating System Interface—UNIX
POTS	Plain Old Telephone Service
PROM	Programmable Read Only Memory
PPP	Point-to-Point Protocol
PSPDN	Packet Switched Public Data Network
PSTN	Public Switched Telephone Network
PTP	Point-to-Point
PU	Physical Unit
PUN	Physical Unit Number

Q

QEB	Query By Example
QoS	Quality of Service

R

RAD	Rapid Application Development
RADSL	Rate Adaptive Digital Subscriber Line
RAID	Redundant Array of Inexpensive Disks
RAM	Random Access Memory
RBOC	Regional Bell Operating Company
RDF	Record Definition Field
RDF (2)	Resource Description Framework
RFC	Request for Comment
RFI	Request for Information
RFP	Request for Proposal
RFS	Remote File System
RIPL	Remote Initial Program Load
RISC	Reduced Instruction Set Computing
RJE	Remote Job Entry
RMF	Remote Management Facility
RND	Remote Name Directory
ROM	Read-Only Memory
RPC	Remote Procedure Call
RSA	Rivest, Shamir, & Adleman (public key encryption technology)
RTF	Rich Text Format
RUP	Relational Unified Process

S

SAN	Storage Area Network
SCSI	Small Computer Systems Interface
S-HTTP	Secure Hypertext Transfer Protocol
SNA	Storage Area Network
SFA	Sales Force Automation
SDLC	Synchronous Data Link Control
SDLC(2)	Systems Development Life Cycle
SDN	Software Defined Network
SDSL	Symmetrical Digital Subscriber Line
SDSL (2)	Single line Digital Subscriber Line
SEC	Securities and Exchange Commission
SET	Secure Electronic Transactions
SGML	Standard Generalized Markup Language

SGMP	Simple Gateway Management Control
SHTTP	Secure Hypertext Transfer Protocol
SIM	Society for Information Management
SIM (2)	Subscriber Identity Module
SIMM	Single In-Line Memory Model
SLA	Service Level Agreement
SLIP	Serial Line Internet Protocol
SMB	Server Message Block
SMDS	Switched Multi-megabit Data Services
S/MIME	Secure Multimedia Internet Mail Extensions
SMB	Server Message Block
SMP	Symmetric Multi Processing
SMS	Strategic Management Society
SMS (2)	Short Message Service
SMS (3)	Storage Management Services
SMTP	Simple Mail Transport Protocol
SNA	System Network Architecture
SNIA	Storage Networking Industry Association
SNMP	Simple Network Management Protocol
SOAP	Simple Object Access Protocol
SOM	System Object Model
SONET	Synchronous Optical Network
SPARC	Scalable Processor ARChitecture
SPARC (2)	Scaleable Performance Architecture
SPOOL	Simultaneous Peripheral Operation On Line
SRI	Stanford Research Institute
SQL	Structured Query Language
SSL	Secure Sockets Layer
S/WAN	Secure Wide-Area Network

T

TAPI	Telephone Application Programming Interface
TB	Terabyte
TCO	Total Cost of Ownership
TCP	Transmission Control Protocol
TCP/IP	Transmission Control Protocol/ Internet Protocol
TDM	Time Division Multiplexing
TDMA	Time Division Multiple Access
TELNET	Telecommunication Network

TFTP	Trivial File Transfer Protocol
TIFF	Tagged Image File Format
TLS	Transport Layer Security
TP	Transaction Processor (monitor)
TP (2)	Transport Protocol
TPA	Trading Partner Agreements
TSAPI	Telephony Server Application Programming Interface
TSO	Time Sharing Option
TWAIN	(*not an acronym*)—It is a scanner interface standard
TXT	Text Format

U

UCITA	Uniform Computer Information Transactions Act
UDDI	Universal Description, Discovery, and Integration
UDP	User Datagram Protocol
UHF	Ultra High Frequency
UML	Unified Modeling Language
UNMA	Unified Network Management Architecture
UPS	Universal Product Code
UPS(2)	Uninterruptible Power Supply
URL	Uniform Resource Locator
USB	Universal Serial Bus
UTP	Unshielded Twisted Pair (cable)

V

VAN	Value-Added Networks
VDSL	Very high data / bit rate Digital Subscriber Line
VF	Voice Frequency Services
VGA	Video Graphics Array
VHF	Very High Frequency
VLSI	Very Large Scale Integration
VM	Virtual Machine
VMS	Virtual Memory System
VoIP	Voice Over Internet Protocol (or Voice over IP)
VPN	Virtual Private Network
VTAM	Virtual Telecommunications Access Method

W

W3C	World Wide Web Consortium
WAN	Wide Area Network
WBEM	Web Based Enterprise Management
WDM	Wavelength Division Multiplexing
WML	Wireless Markup Language
WORM	Write Once Read Many
WSDL	Web Services Description Language
WYSIWYG	What You See Is What You Get

X

XML	Extensible Markup Language
XMP	X/Open Management Protocol
XMS	Extended Memory Specifications
XNP	Extended Network Protocol
XP	eXtreme Programming

Registered Trademarks

Some of the glossary & acronyms in this publication are registered trademarks of the Crown Copyright Office of Government Commerce. They are reproduced with the permission of the Controller of HMSO and the Office of Government Commerce.

ITIL is a registered trademark, and a registered community trademark of the Office of Government Commerce, and is registered in the U.S. Patent and Trademark Office.

PRINCE is a registered trademark and a registered community trademark of the Office of Government Commerce, and is registered in the U.S. Patent and Trademark Office.

M_o_R® is a registered trademark and a registered community trademark of the Office of Government Commerce.

Windows and Microsoft Exchange are registered trademarks of the Microsoft Corporation.

ZDNet News is a registered trademark of CNET Networks.

Star Trek is a registered trademark of Paramount Pictures Corporation. All Rights Reserved.

Reference Material

Reference Books

Allen, Cliff, et. al. *Guide to One-To-One Web Marketing*. New York: John Wiley & Sons, Inc., 1998.

Bossidy, Larry and Ram Charan. *Execution: The Discipline of Getting Things Done*. New York: Crown Business, 2002.

Cerami, Ethan. *Web Services Essentials*. California: O'Reilly & Associates, Inc., 2002.

Collins, Jim. *Good To Great*. New York: HarperCollins Publishers, Inc., 2001.

Courtney, Hugh, et al. *Harvard Business Review on Managing Uncertainty*. Boston: Harvard Business School Press, 1999.

Covey, Stephen. *The 8th Habit*. New York: Free Press, a Division of Simon & Schuster, Inc., 2004.

Covey, Stephen. *The 7 Habits of Highly Effective People*. New York: Simon & Schuster, Inc., 1989.

Foster, Richard and Sarah Kaplan. *Creative Destruction: Why Companies That Are Built To Last Underperform The Market And How To Successfully Transform Them*. New York: Currency/Doubleday, 2001.

Grady, Robert B. and Deborah L. Caswell. *Software Metrics: Establishing a company-wide program*. New Jersey P T R Prentice-Hall, Inc., 1987.

Hesselbein, F. and P. M. Cohen. *Leader to Leader*. San Francisco: Jossey-Bass, 1999.

Hill, Napoleon. *Law of Success*. Chicago: Success Unlimited, Inc., 1979.

Johnson, Craig E. *Meeting the Ethical Challenges of Leadership: Casting light or shadow*. Thousand Oaks, CA: Sage Publications, Inc., 2005.

Josephson, Michael. *Making Ethical Decisions*. Los Angeles: Josephson Institute of Ethics, 2002.

Kaplan, Robert S. and David P. Norton. *The Balanced Scorecard: Translating Strategy into Action.* Harvard Business School Press, 1996.

Kaplan, Robert S. and David P. Norton. *The Strategy-Focused Organization: How Balanced Scorecard Companies Thrive in the New Business Environment.* Boston: Harvard Business School Press, 2001.

Kidder, Rushworth M.. *Moral Courage.* New York: HarperCollins Publishers, Inc., 2005.

King, Roger. *Object-Oriented Concepts, Databases, and Applications.* New York: ACM Press, 1989.

Kosiur, David. *Understanding Electronic Commerce.* Redmond: Microsoft Press, 1997.

Marks, Eric A. and Mark J. Werrell. *Executive Guide to Web Services.* New Jersey: John Wiley & Sons, Inc., 2003.

Marshall, Edward M. *Building Trust at the Speed of Change: The Power of the Relationship-Based Corporation.* New York: AMACOM, American Management Association, 2000.

Martin, James. *Rapid Application Development.* Englewood Cliffs: Prentice-Hall, 1992.

Nelson, Bob. *1001 Ways to Reward Employees.* New York: Workman Publishing Company, 1994.

Newcomer, Eric. *Understanding Web Services.* Boston: Addison-Wesley, 2002.

Noland, Dr. Richard L. *Managing the Data Resource Function.* New York: West Publishing Co., 1974.

Pinchot III, Gifford. *Intrapreneuring: Why You Don't Have to Leave the Corporation to Become an Entrepreneur.* New York: Harper & Row, 1985.

Schwartz, Peter. *The Art of the Long View: Paths to Strategic Insight for Yourself and Your Company.* New York: Doubleday, 1991.

Smith, Hyrum W. *What Matters Most: The Power of Living Your Values.* New York: Franklin Covey Company, 2000.

Sterne, Jim. *World Wide Web Marketing.* New York: John Wiley & Sons, Inc., 1999.

Werrell, Mark J. and Eric A. Marks. *Executive Guide to Web Services.* New Jersey: John Wiley & Sons, Inc., 2003.

Yourdon, Ed. *Managing the Structured Techniques.* New York: Yourdon Press, 1976.

Yourdon, Ed. *Modern Structured Analysis.* New York: Yourdon Press, 1988.

Books Recommended by CIOs

Bennis, W. *On Becoming A Leader: The Leadership Classic—Updated & Expanded.* Cambridge: Perseus Publishing, 2003.

Bergmann, H., et al. *Everyone a Leader: A Grassroots Model for the New Workplace.* New York: John Wiley & Sons, Inc., 1999.

Blanchard, K., et al. *Leadership By the Book: Tools to Transform Your Workplace.* New York: William Morrow & Company, Inc., 1999.

Bossidy, Larry and Ram Charan. *Execution: The Discipline of Getting Things Done.* New York: Crown Business, 2002.

Brin, D. *The Transparent Society: Will Technology Force Us To Choose Between Privacy & Freedom?* New York: Perseus Books, 1998.

Buckingham, M. and C. Coffman. *First, Break All The Rules: What the World's Greatest Managers Do Differently.* New York: Simon & Schuster, 1999.

Byham, W. C. *Zapp! The Lightning of Empowerment: How to Improve Productivity, Quality, and Employee Satisfaction.* New York: The Ballantine Publishing Group, 1998.

Collins, James C. and Jerry I. Porras. *Built To Last: Successful Habits of Visionary Companies.* New York: HarperCollins, 2002.

Collins, Jim. *Good To Great.* New York: HarperCollins Publishers, Inc., 2001.

Copper, K. *The Relational Enterprise: Moving Beyond CRM to Maximize All Your Business Relationships.* New York: American Management Association, 2002.

Covey, Stephen. *The 7 Habits of Highly Effective People.* New York: Simon & Schuster, Inc., 1989.

Davenport, T. H. and L. Prusak. *What is The Big Idea?: Creating and Capitalizing on the Best New Management Thinking.* Boston: Harvard Business School Publishing, 2003.

Demarco, T. *The Deadline: A Novel About Project Management.* New York: Dorset House Publishing, 1997.

Gates, B. *Business @ the Speed of Thought: Succeeding In The Digital Economy.* New York: Warner Books, Inc., 1999.

Hammer, M. *The Agenda.* New York: Crown Business, 2001.

Hochberg, I. *Who Stole My Cheese?!!: An A-Mazing Way to Make More Money From the Poor Suckers That You Cheated in Your Work And In Your Life.* Philadelphia: Running Press Book Publishers, 2003.

Kelly, K. *The Secret Handshake: Mastering the Politics of the Business Inner Circle.* New York: Currency, 2000.

MacKay, H. *Dig Your Well Before You're Thirsty: The Only Networking Book You'll Ever Need.* New York: Currency, 1997.

MacKay, H. *Beware the Naked Man Who Offers You His Shirt: Do What You Love, Love What You Do, And Deliver More Than You Promise.* New York: Ballantine Books, 1990.

Maxwell, J. C. *The 21 Irrefutable Laws of Leadership.* Tennessee: Thomas Nelson, Inc., 1998.

Musashi, M. and T. Cleary (translator). *The Book of Five Rings.* Boston: Shambhala, 2005.

Peters, T. *Thriving On Chaos: Handbook for a Management Revolution.* New York: HarperCollins Publishers, 1987.

Schwarzkopf, N. *It Doesn't Take a Hero: The Autobiography of General H. Norman Schwarzkopf.* Bantam, 1993.

Smart, B. D. *Topgrading: How Leading Companies Win By Hiring, Coaching, and Keeping the Best People.* New York: Penquin Group, 2005.

Tapscott, D. and D. Ticoll. *The Naked Corporation: How the Age of Transparency Will Revolutionize Business.* New York: Free Press, 2003.

Tichy, Noel M. *The Leadership Engine: How Winning Companies Build Leadership at Every Level.* New York: HarperBusiness, 1997.

Tzu, Sun. *The Art of War.* Philadelphia: Running Press Book Publishers, 2003.

What are the top three books that you would recommend for a new CIO to read?

"I don't have any recommendations for specific books; however, consider a book about integrating IT strategy with business strategy. You should also consider books about negotiation skills and integrating Web solutions into corporate business processes."

Terry Miller
Professor of eCommerce
Kaplan University

Web sites and Magazines

The following are a list of Web sites and magazines that have information that is helpful for any CIO. Many of the magazines are free publications to IT professionals.

1. **Agile Alliance, The**—http://www.agilealliance.com/—The **Agile Alliance** is a non-profit organization that supports individuals and organizations that use agile approaches to develop software.

2. **Association for Computing Machinery (ACM)**—http://www.acm.org/— ACM was founded in 1947. Its purpose is to advance the skills of information technology professionals and students worldwide. This organization has about 80,000 members. It provides a portal to a great deal of computing literature and publications.

3. *Baseline* **Magazine**—The bottom line in IT—is a guide to planning, costing, and managing the implementation of IT solutions to baseline results. From the financial aspects of IT deployment (ROI) to the actual implementation of the IT infrastructure that support mission critical corporate goals and objectives.

4. *Bio-IT World* **Magazine**—*Bio-IT World* is a new publication that is focused on technology for the life sciences. It is a monthly publication from International Data Group (IDG) that helps professionals in the life sciences industries. It provides editorial coverage of technology systems, products, and services created specifically for the life science applications.

5. **Carnegie Mellon's CIO Institute**—http://cioi.web.cmu.edu/—Carnegie Mellon's Chief Information Officer Institute is a leader in IT executive education. The CIO Institute provides concentrated professional education programs for current and future information executives. An IT executive can work towards a Federal CIO certification.

6. *CIO*—http://www.cio.com/—*CIO* the magazine and CIO.com are published by CXO Media Inc. Its purpose is to meet the needs of informa-

tion executives. The *CIO* magazine is read by more than 140,000 CIOs and senior executives.

7. *CIO Insight*—http://www.cioinsight.com/—*CIO Insight* is a business journal for senior IT decision-makers. Its mission is "to provide the IT elite with articles about the cutting-edge strategies, management techniques and technology perspectives they need to succeed in the digital economy."

8. ***Database Trends and Applications* Magazine**—*Database Trends and Applications* is a monthly publication providing corporate information projects teams with coverage of the technology, intelligence, and insight needed to conceptualize, plan, initiate, implement, and manage large-scale, integrated-information-rich projects.

9. **Desktop Pipeline**—http://www.desktoppipeline.com/—Desktop Pipeline provides information to IT professionals that help them manage enterprise desktop technologies. The Web site contains product, vendor, and financial news; trends, feature stories, and case studies; how-to columns, best practices, as well as product reviews.

10. **Geek.com**—http://www.geek.com—An online technology resource for IT professionals. The Geek.com Web site states that it was created to fill a gaping hole on the Internet. It describes itself as being a place that geeks can call home and where those who aspire to be geeks can get their feet wet.

11. **Information Technology Infrastructure Library (ITIL)**—http://www.itil.co.uk/index.htm—The Information Technology Infrastructure Library (ITIL) is a set of guidance developed by the United Kingdom's Office of Government Commerce (OGC). It is essentially a de facto standard that is a set of best practices for managing the processes required to effectively manage the delivery of IT services and support.

12. *InformationWeek*—*InformationWeek*, the magazine, is printed weekly and is read by approximately 440,000 technology professionals at more

than a quarter million unique locations. It provides a perspective and in-depth analysis on news, research, and IT trends. Their mission is to help business technology professionals drive business innovation.

13. **InformationWeek.com**—http://www.informationweek.com/— Informationweek.com delivers news, a comprehensive array of propri-etary *InformationWeek* research, as well as analysis on IT trends, a white paper library, and original editorial content, all designed to complement our print publication in a 24/7 environment.

14. **InfoWorld**—http://www.infoworld.com/—*InfoWorld* magazine is a resource for IT experts who are responsible for making technology-buy-ing decisions. It contains product comparisons, analyses, and reviews. There are features on technology issues, opinions, and advice from columnists.

15. *Insurance & Technology*—*Insurance & Technology* provides insurance decision-makers with the information they need to get a return on the technology investments required to advance corporate business strate-gies. It provides business technology professionals with topics that range from technology coverage and analysis, to perspectives on the latest trends that help achieve businesses and customer value.

16. *Intelligent Enterprise*—http://www.intelligententerprise.com/—*Intelligent Enterprise* is a magazine dedicated to helping an organization plan and deploy strategic business applications that turn information into intelli-gence. *Intelligent Enterprise* empowers business application strategists who are responsible for the value of strategic information within their enter-prises.

17. **InternetWeek.com**—http://internetweek.cmp.com/—InternetWeek covers the business and technology of the Internet and allows the reader to probe as deep as they need to. Daily, it delivers breaking news, fea-tures, polls, and reviews on upcoming technologies and trends.

18. *IT Architect*—*IT Architect* is an IT publication dedicated to the critical decisions of technology architecture. Each month, it provides an assessment of the risks and benefits of technology.

19. *KM World*—http://www.kmworld.com/—The *KM World* magazine and Web site provides news, articles, white papers, and reviews on content, documents, and knowledge management.

20. **Linux Pipeline**—http://www.linuxpipeline.com/—Linux Pipeline provides intelligence, hands-on experience, and insights into harnessing Linux and open-source applications in the enterprise. The site provides articles, columns, reviews, tutorials, and news that help enterprises find or build the right applications to solve problems and show a return on the IT investment.

21. *Managing Automation*—*Managing Automation* provides a set of decision-support informational tools for manufacturers. It is designed for companies who are using information and automation technologies to transform their businesses to create a competitive advantage.

22. **Methodology.org**—http://www.methodology.org—Methodology.org is a Web site that provides IT developers and programmers with methodology resources, documents, and tools. Its intention is to bridge the gap between methodology scholars and rapid development professionals. This site is a part of the itmWEB network of Internet sites.

23. **Mobile Pipeline**—http://www.mobilepipeline.com/—Mobile Pipeline provides news, reviews, product announcements, product research tools, advice and analysis, and insights into industry trends.

24. *Network Computing*—*Network Computing* provides analysis of technologies, vendors, and products to IT managers and staff who are accountable for strategic technology purchase decisions.

25. *Optimize*—*Optimize* provides IT senior management and technology-involved CXOs with business-thought leadership and practical knowledge to bridge the gap between business strategy and IT execution.

26. Outsourcing Center, The—http://www.outsourcing-center.com/—Outsourcing Center is an Internet portal for information on methods for creating and sustaining information about the outsourcing business and marketplace.

27. *Secure Enterprise*—*Secure Enterprise* provides analysis and advice based on its product evaluations to IT security professionals. It's a decision-maker's tool for the information security professional.

28. *Software Development*—*Software Development* magazine helps IT and business leaders to develop, manage, and purchase enterprise-wide software development projects. Each issue is designed to provide IT and development managers with leadership guidance over the management of difficult IT solutions. This magazine targets corporate developers and technical managers working at companies with substantial development staffs.

29. *Storage Pipeline*—*Storage Pipeline* evaluates technologies and analyzes vendors, products, trends, and issues. It assesses the direction of the industry, explores new standards and developments, and provides a real-world view on vendor strategy.

30. Systems Management Pipeline—http://www.systemsmanagementpipeline.com/ —Systems Management Pipeline provides IT professionals with the information to manage their organization's hardware, software, peripherals, and networking. This Web site delivers news, trends, buyers' guides, how-to information, and analysis.

31. TechRepublic.com—http://techrepublic.com/—a member of CNET Networks that provides interactive online content across a family of brands, of which TechRepublic.com is one.

32. **TechWeb.com**— http://www.techweb.com/— TechWeb is a network of tech sites, providing information and marketing services to the builders, sellers, and users of technology worldwide.

33. ***Wall Street & Technology***—*Wall Street & Technology* provides information, news, trends, and strategy that business and IT leaders in the securities and investment markets need to make intelligent technology decisions.

34. **Webopedia**—http://www.webopedia.com/—An online dictionary and search engine for computer and Internet technology definitions.

35. **Wikipedia**—http://en.wikipedia.org/—Wikipedia is a free online encyclopedia that anyone can edit.

36. **ZDNet News**—http://news.zdnet.com—a member of CNET Networks that provides interactive online content across a family of brands, of which ZDNet News is one.

Other References

"Diagnostic and Statistical Manual of Mental Disorders", Fourth Edition, Text Revision. Washington, DC, American Psychiatric Association, 2000.

"On Managing Uncertainty." *Harvard Business Review.* Boston: Harvard Business School Publishing Corporation, 1999.

"On Motivating People." *Harvard Business Review.* Boston: Harvard Business School Publishing Corporation, 2003.

Index

"What act that roars so loud, and thunders in the index?"

—William Shakespeare (*Hamlet. Act iii. Sc. 4.*)

Index

Not A CIO?—Read This

Do you have a need to understand what a CIO does ... or should do?

Then you should be aware that ...
Unwrapping the CIO: Demystifying the Chief Information Officer Position
Is Not Just for CIOs

If You Are A ...

Chief Executive Officer/Chief Operations Officer who is depending more and more on information technology for the success of your business and you need to have a CIO that understands the technology as well as possesses the leadership skills to work well at the senior management level...If you need to understand the key components of the CIO function, or you just need to understand the position better to select the right CIO for the job...then *Unwrapping the CIO: Demystifying the Chief Information Officer Position* is what you need.

Business Unit Manager who must interact with the CIO on a daily basis and you have a need to better understand of the CIO position...If you need to understand the key components of the CIO function to work more efficiently with the CIO...then *Unwrapping the CIO: Demystifying the Chief Information Officer Position* will help you to have a better grasp of the function and the person.

Chief Financial Officer who needs a detailed understanding of the areas of IT that affect the finances of the company or if you need to understand the key operational components of the IT function...If you must recognize the areas of the CIO function that have an impact on the major operations of the business...then *Unwrapping the CIO: Demystifying the Chief Information Officer Position* is a must-read for you.

Chief Technology Officer/CIO who needs a way to communicate the significant aspects of your job to those who don't quite understand your multitude of challenges…If you need to understand when to be a technologist and when to be a business person…If you are a new CIO who needs to better understand the job that you're taking on or you need to understand the skills that are required to be both effective and successful at your job…then *Unwrapping the CIO: Demystifying the Chief Information Officer Position* should be kept in your briefcase!

Information Technology Professional who has a career path that includes becoming a CIO…If you don't quite understand the decisions that the CIO makes and need to better understand the reasons behind those decisions…If you need to enhance your working relationship with the CIO of your company…then *Unwrapping the CIO: Demystifying the Chief Information Officer Position* is required reading in achieving the goal of becoming a CIO or understanding how to work with your current CIO.

About the Author

Wayne L. Anderson is the president and chief IT strategist of Anderson Professional Systems Group, LLC (http://www.apsg-ltd.com) an IT management consulting company that he founded. He provides coaching to senior managers on the CIO function. He frequently speaks on the topic of how to be successful in the CIO position. In addition, he speaks on how to create a successful information organization. He has been a keynote speaker at a number of professional organizations and academic institutions.

Mr. Anderson has over thirty years in the information technology (IT) industry. He's been a senior IT executive for the past fifteen years. He is a senior executive with an equal blend of technical, business, and managerial skills developed during experience with several Fortune 500 companies. He has held the position of senior vice president of IT—as well as divisional CIO—for several multibillion-dollar corporations. He works with CIOs and corporations to further their long- and short-range business goals. He provides extensive experience in managing multimillion-dollar budgets and large professional IT staffs. Mr. Anderson also possesses the unique ability to attract, retain, and motivate outstanding management and professional personnel.

Mr. Anderson is active in professional organizations such as the Association for Systems Management (ASM), Society for Information Management (SIM), and the Project Management Institute (PMI). He has served on the board of directors of ASM. He holds the designation of Certified Systems Professional (CSP).

In addition, Mr. Anderson is a member of the Board of Directors of Entrepreneurs of Tulsa.

Mr. Anderson is available for speaking engagements. In addition, you may connect with Mr. Anderson through his professional network on LinkedIn.com using the URL address http://www.linkedin.com/in/ciounwrapped.

978-0-595-40058-4
0-595-40058-2

Printed in the United States
77942LV00005B/101

9 780595 400584